CHICKEN THOUGHTS

COMICS ABOUT BIRDS

Look for Chicken Thoughts on your favorite social media site!

ISBN: 978-1-0878-8873-6 (hardcover)
ISBN: 978-1-0878-8874-3 (ebook)

for Mom, Dad, Anna and Jordan

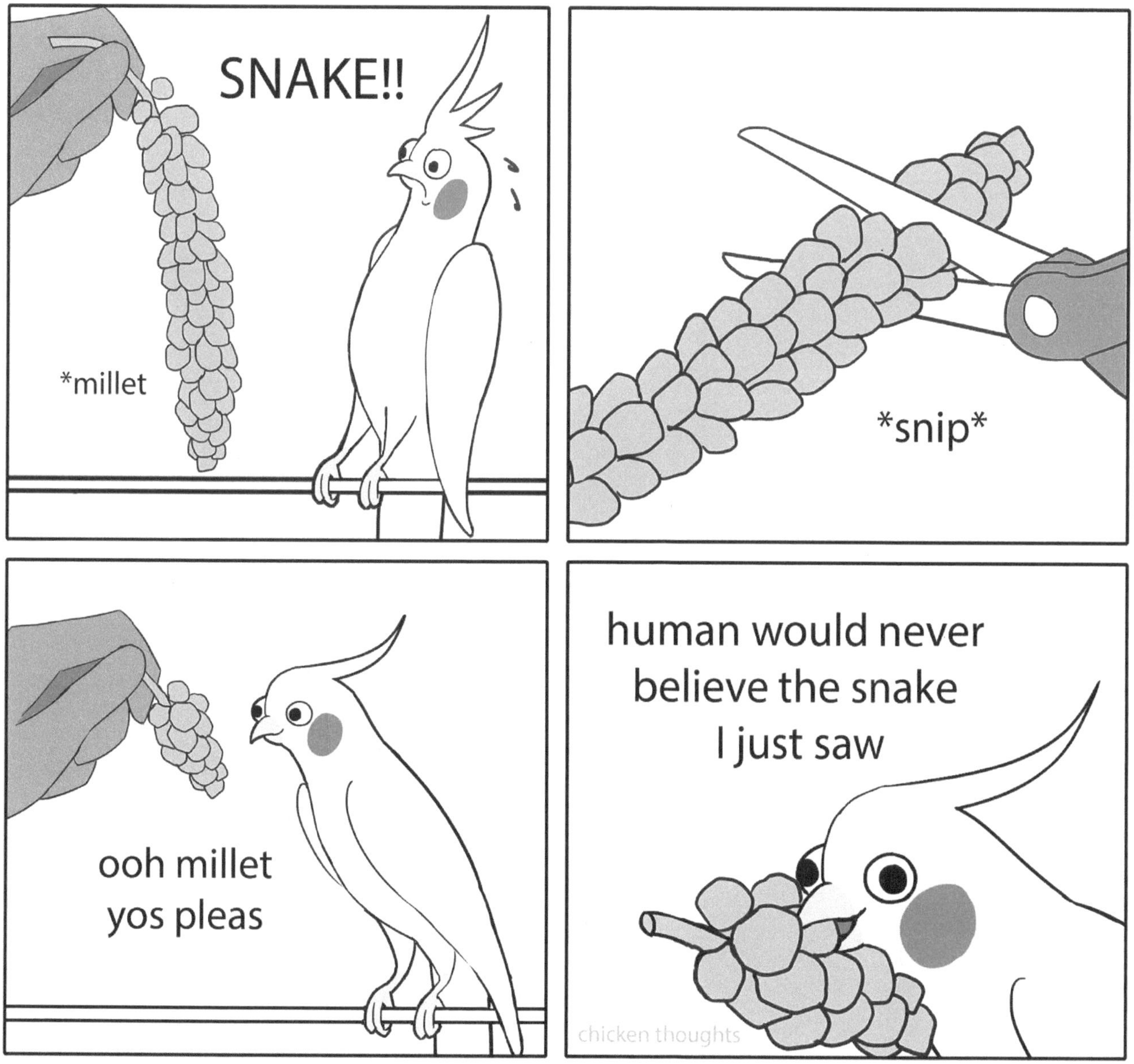
SNAKE!!
*millet
snip
ooh millet
yos pleas
human would never
believe the snake
I just saw
chicken thoughts

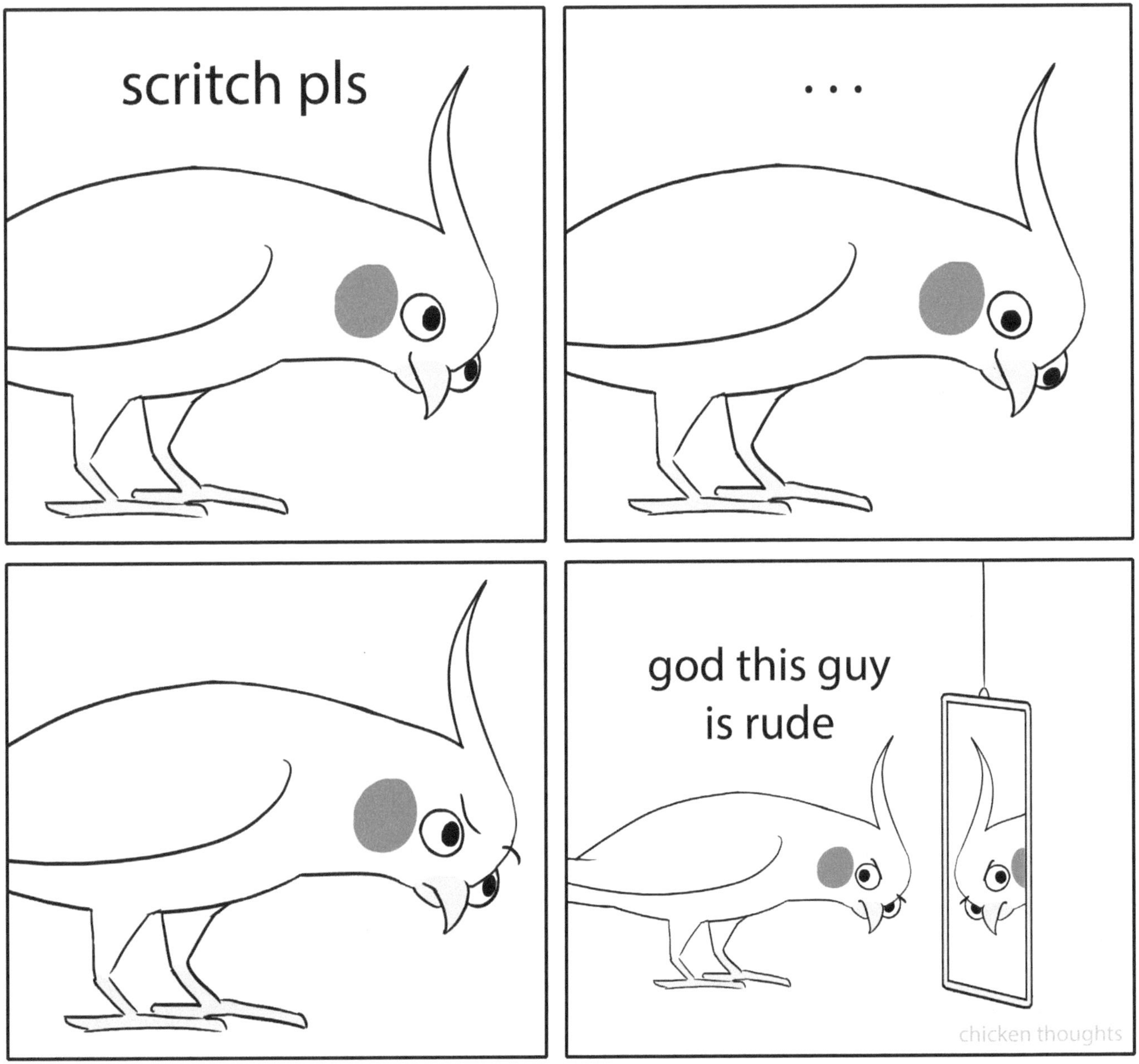
scritch pls
...
god this guy
is rude
chicken thoughts

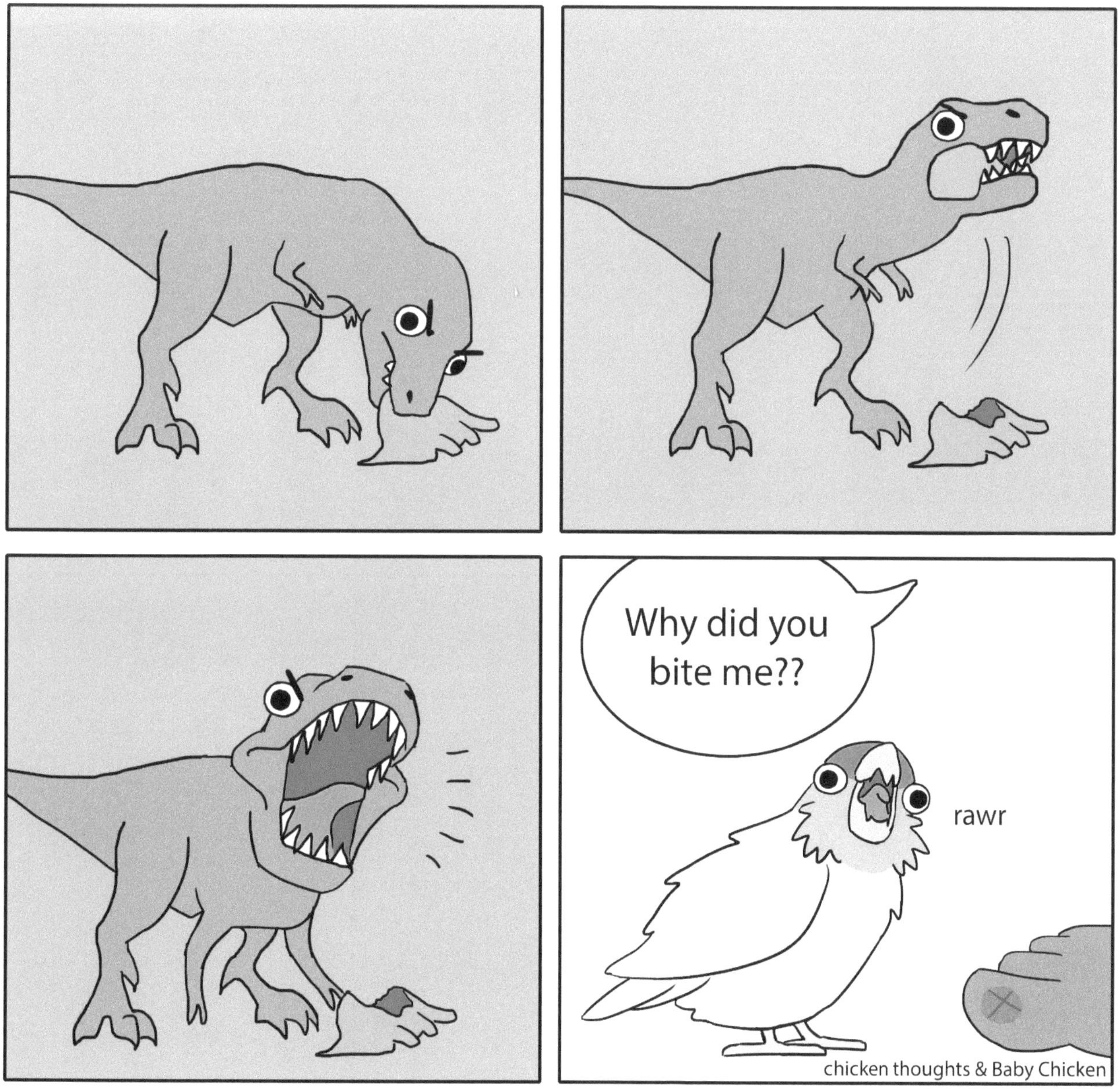
Why did you bite me??
rawr
chicken thoughts & Baby Chicken

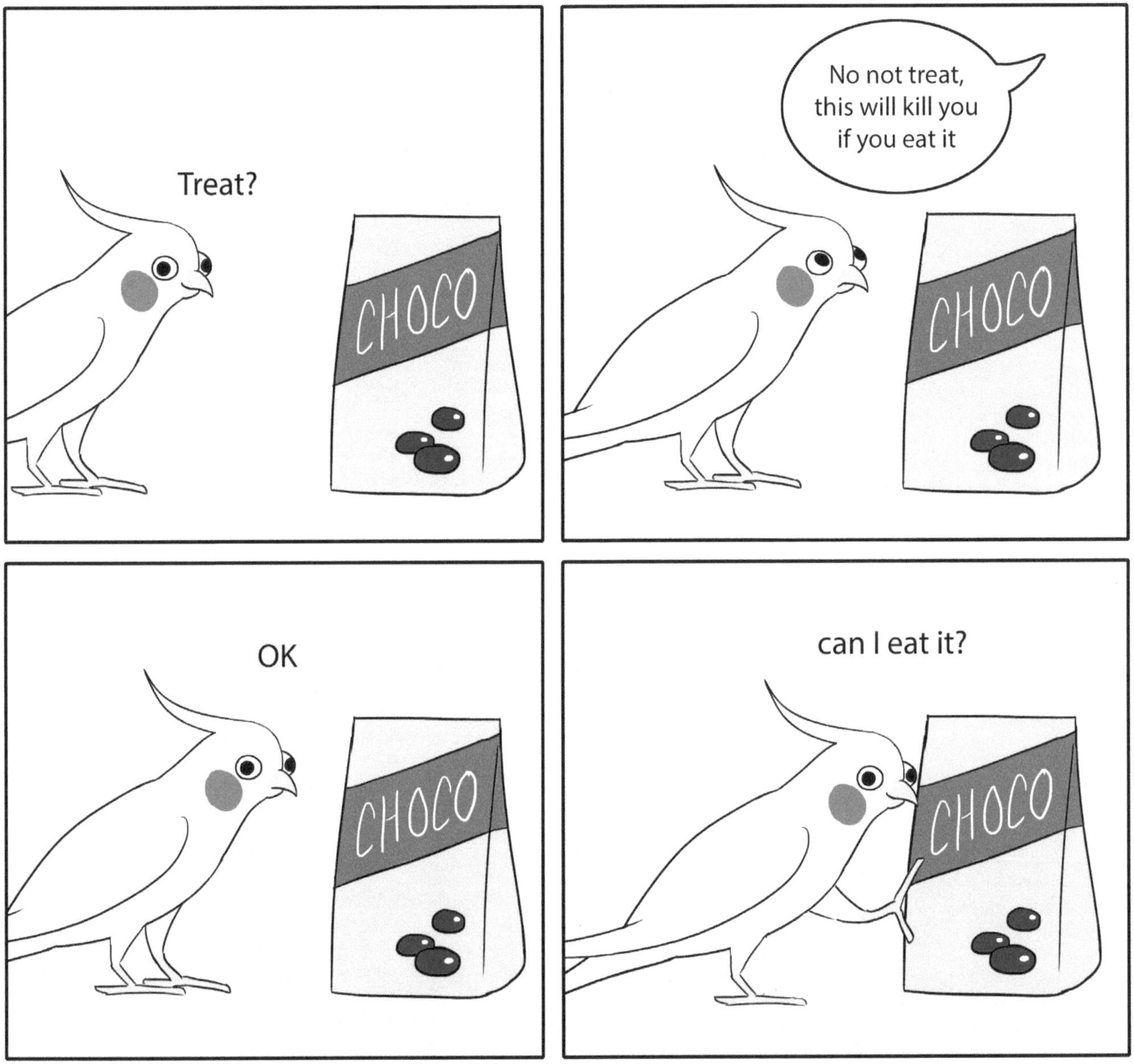
Treat?
CHOCO
No not treat, this will kill you if you eat it
CHOCO
OK
CHOCO
can I eat it?
CHOCO

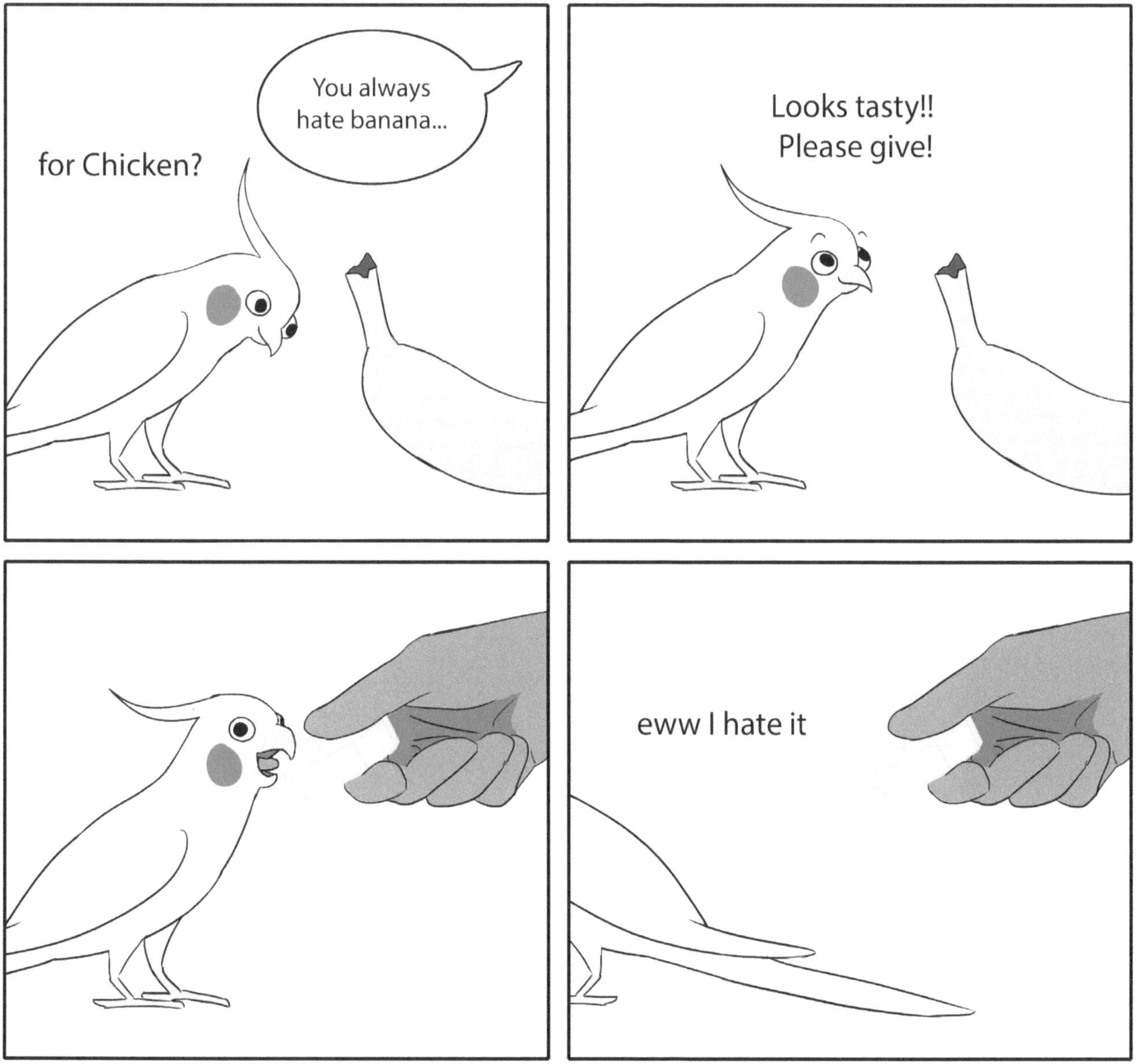
for Chicken?
You always hate banana...
Looks tasty!! Please give!
eww I hate it

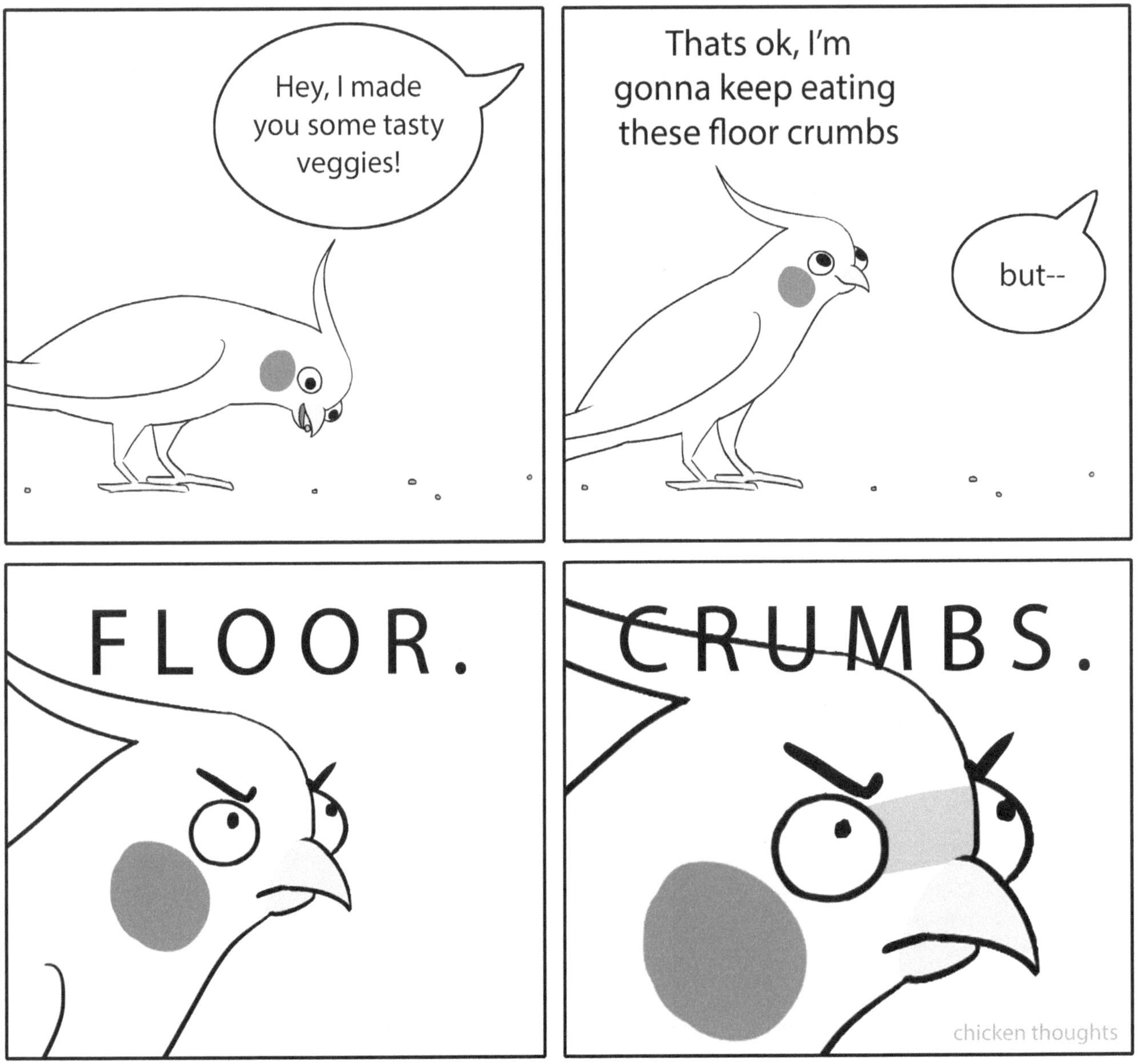
Hey, I made you some tasty veggies!
Thats ok, I'm gonna keep eating these floor crumbs
but--
FLOOR.
CRUMBS.
chicken thoughts

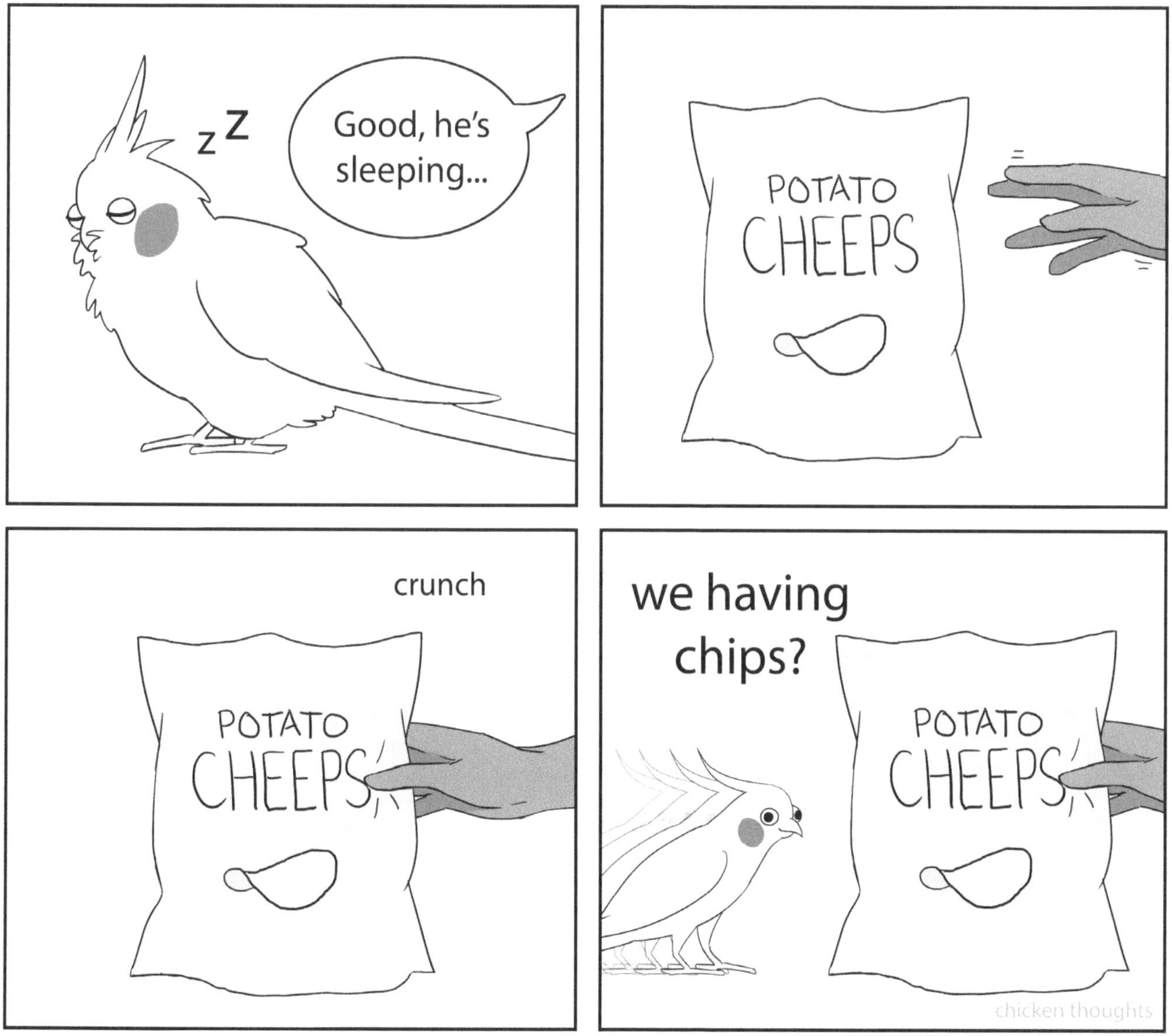
z Z
Good, he's sleeping...
POTATO CHEEPS
crunch
POTATO CHEEPS
we having chips?
POTATO CHEEPS
chicken thoughts

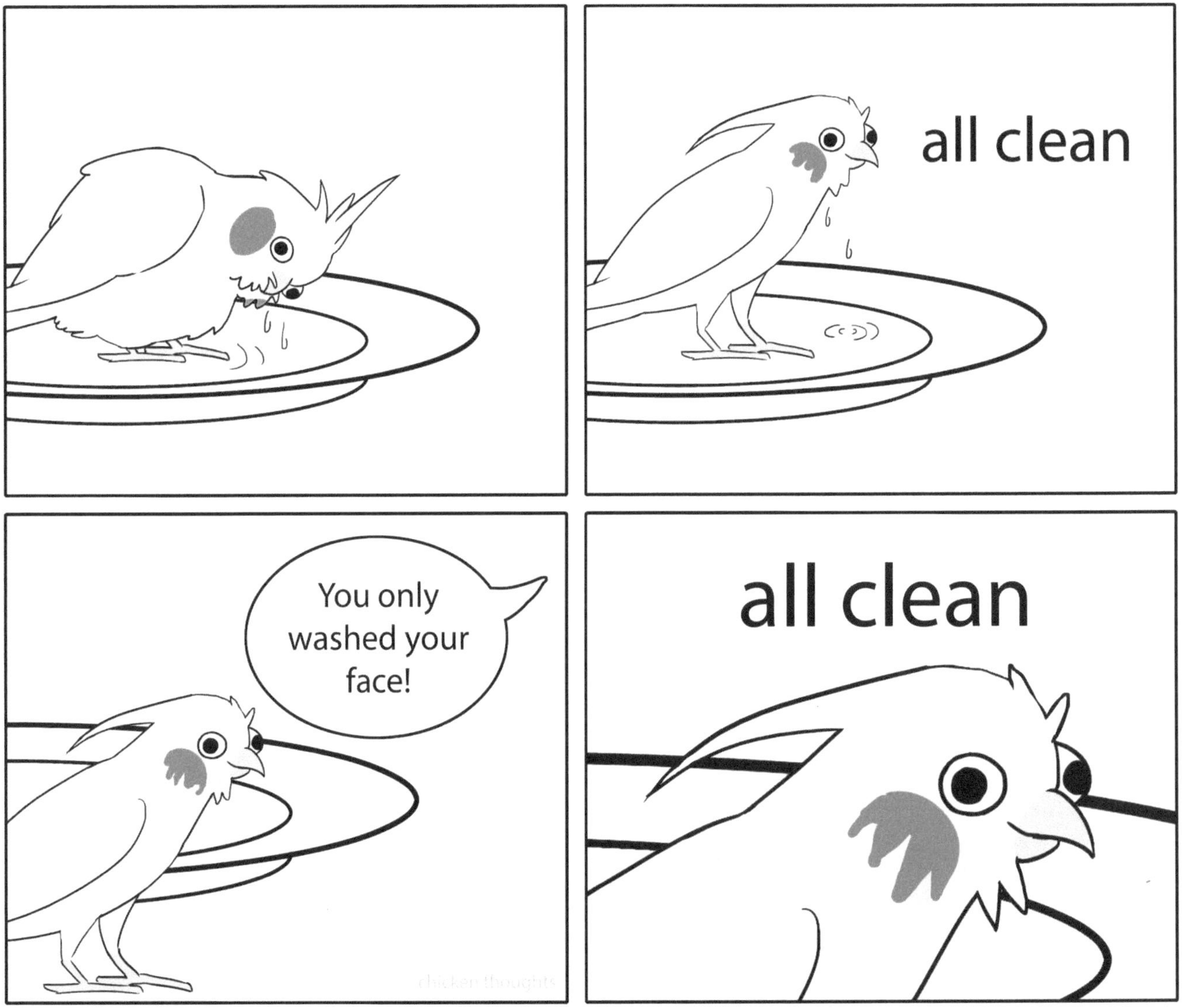
all clean
You only washed your face!
chicken thoughts
all clean

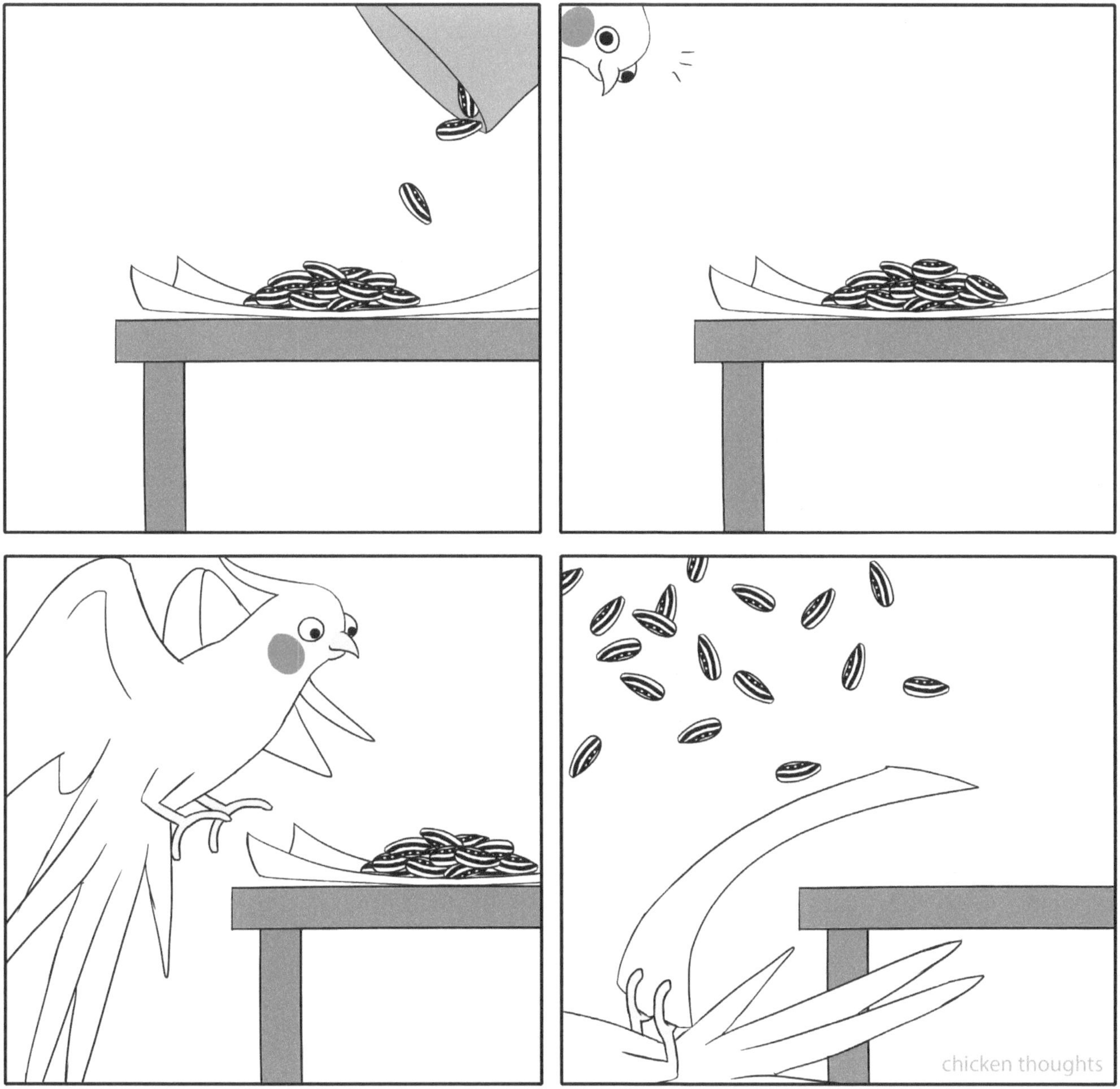
chicken thoughts

small mishap
no problem
I got this
everything's fine
chicken thoughts

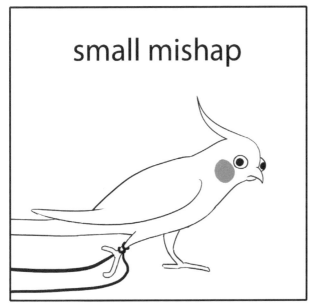

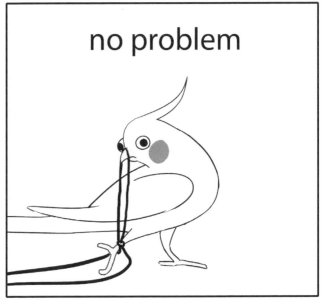

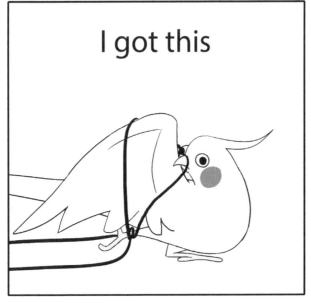

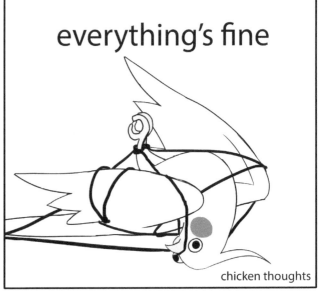

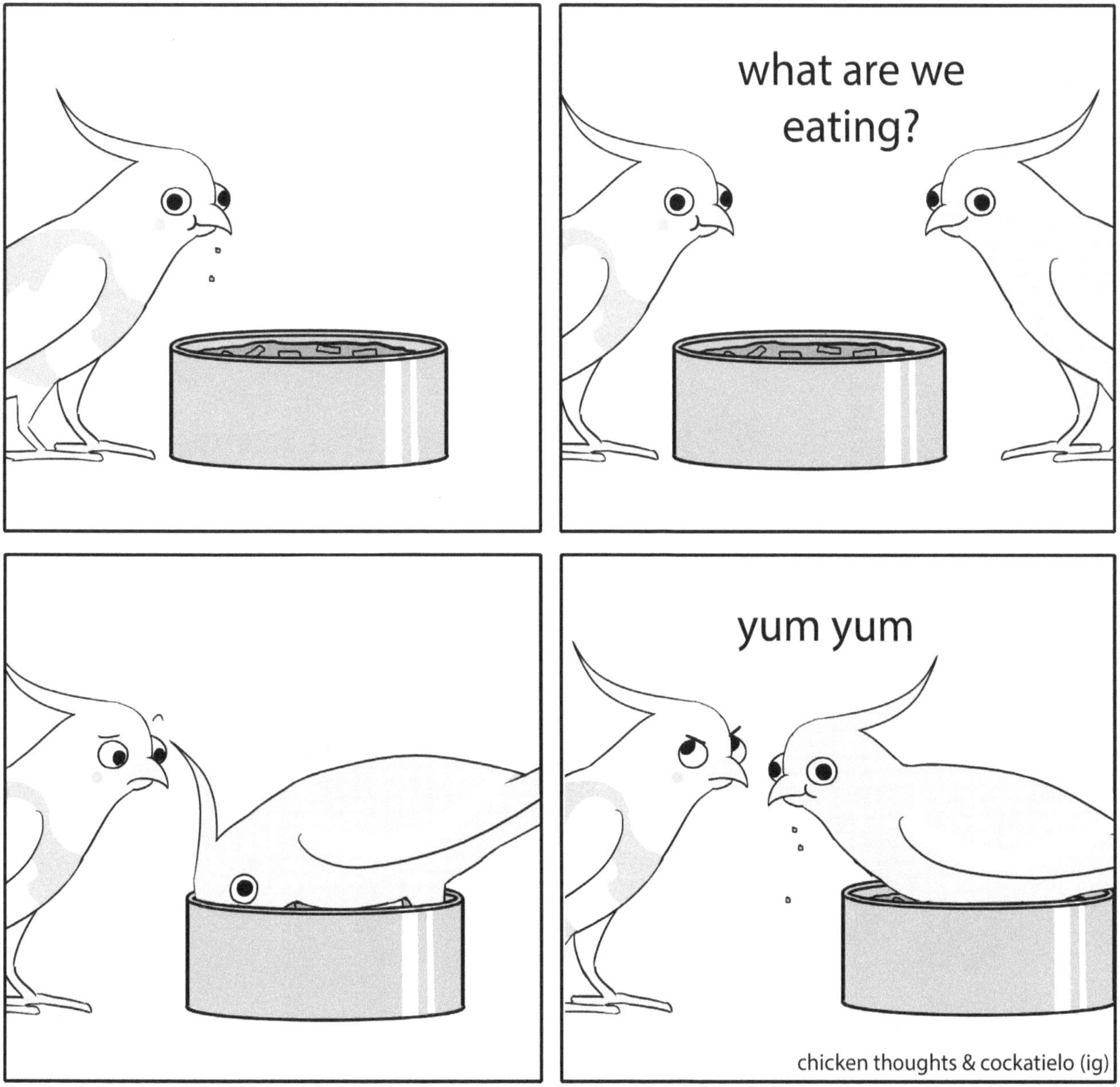
what are we eating?
yum yum
chicken thoughts & cockatielo (ig)

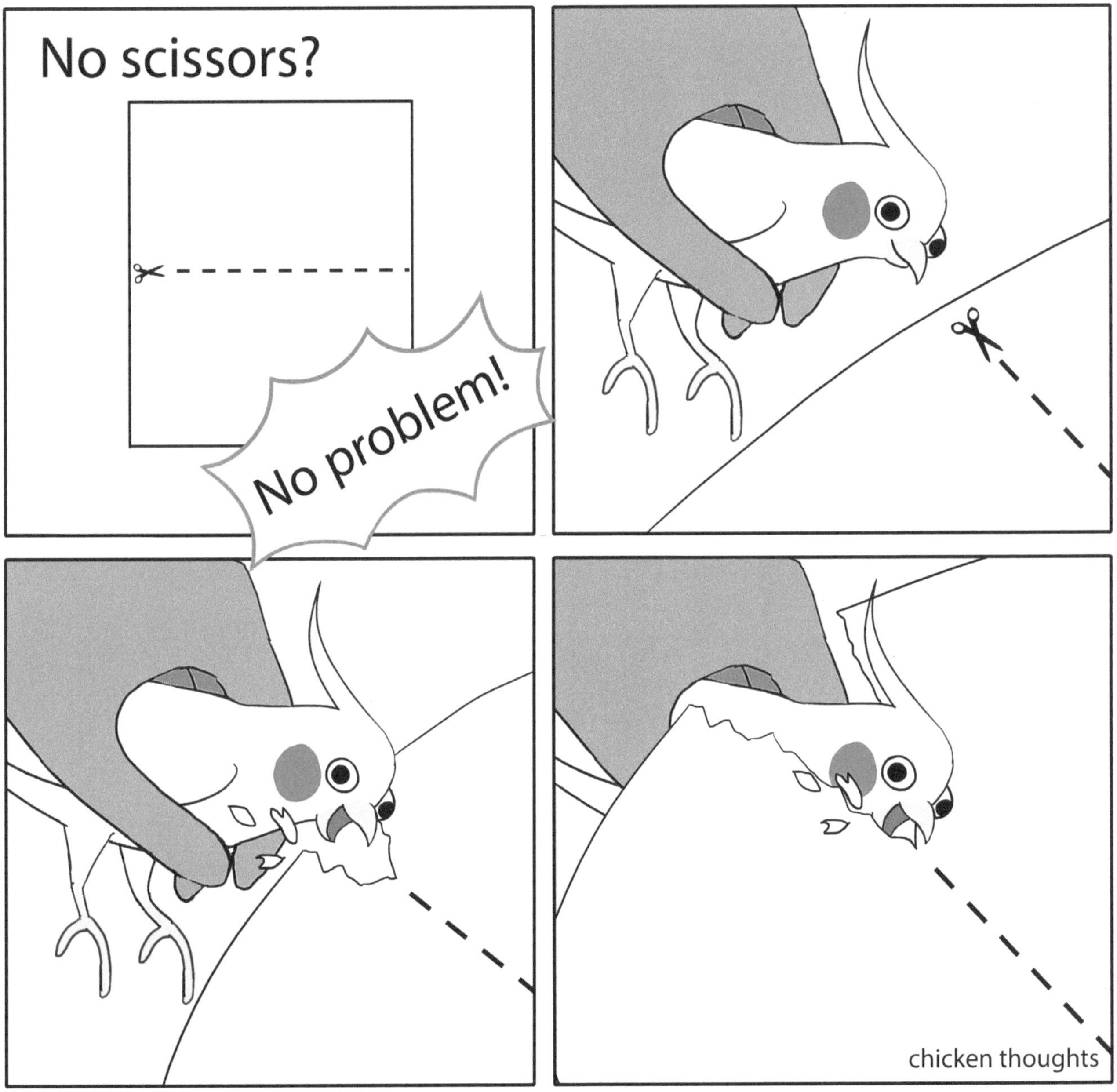
No scissors?
No problem!
chicken thoughts

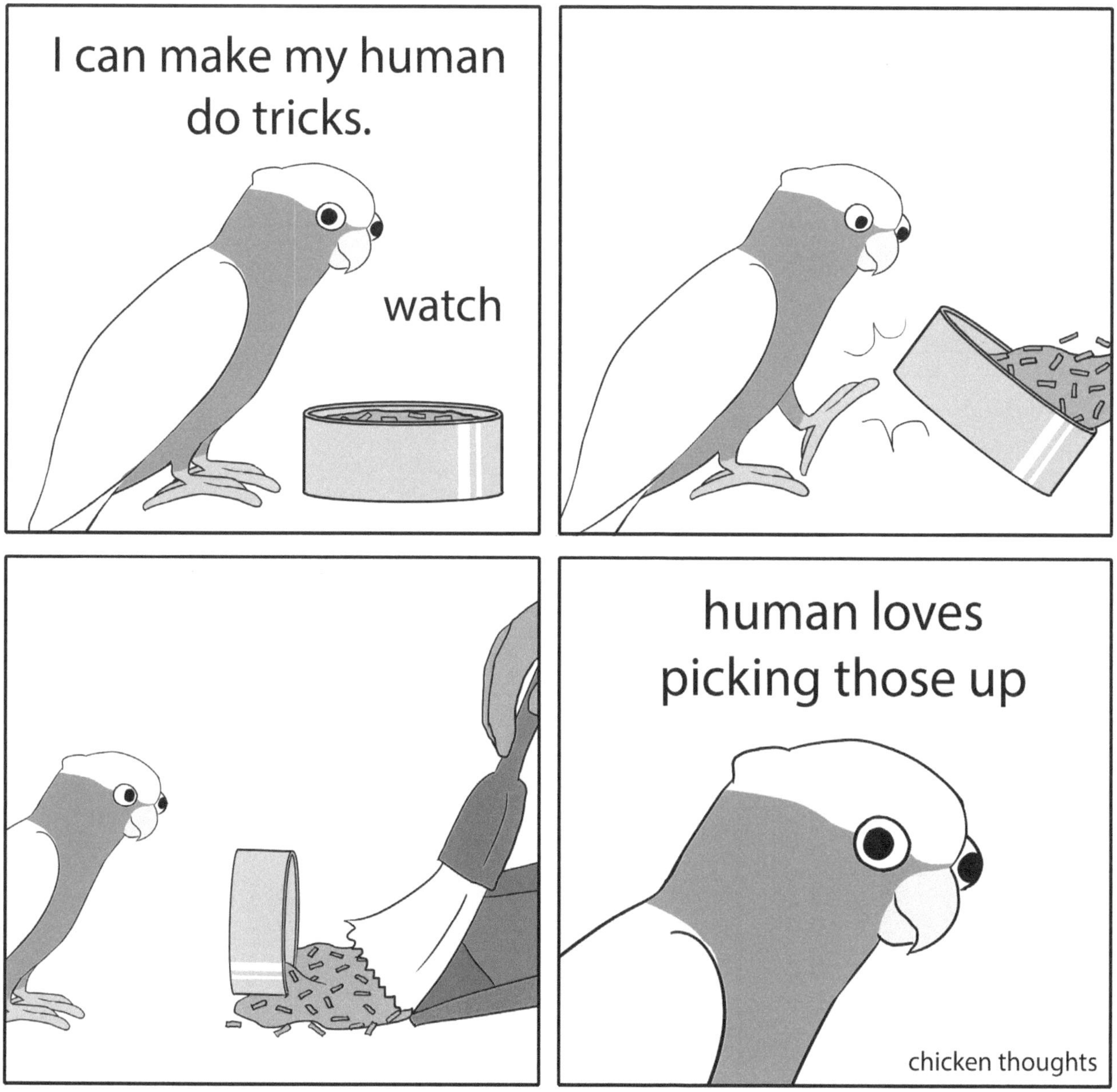
I can make my human do tricks.
watch
human loves picking those up
chicken thoughts

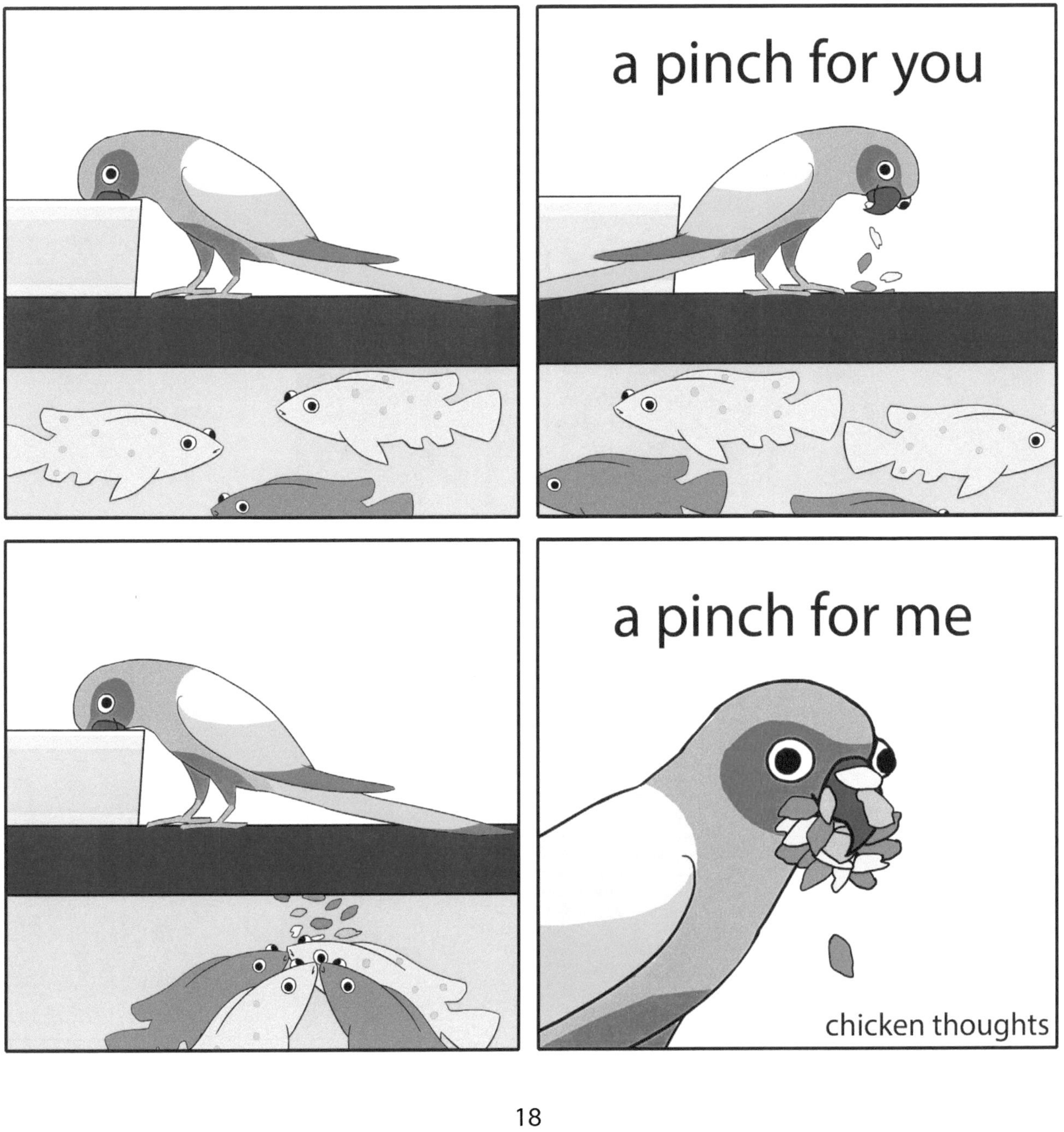
a pinch for you
a pinch for me
chicken thoughts

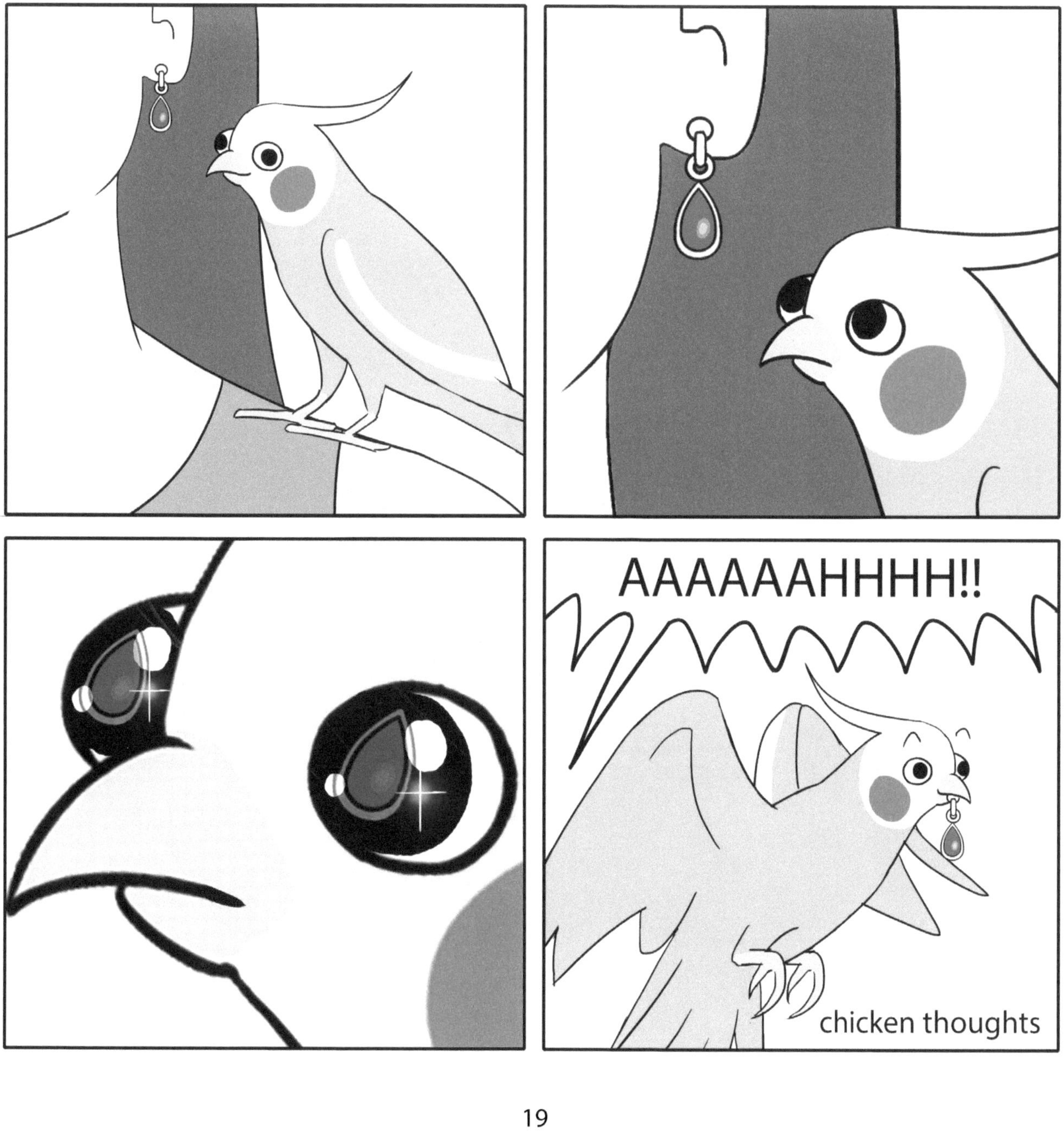
AAAAAAHHHH!!
chicken thoughts

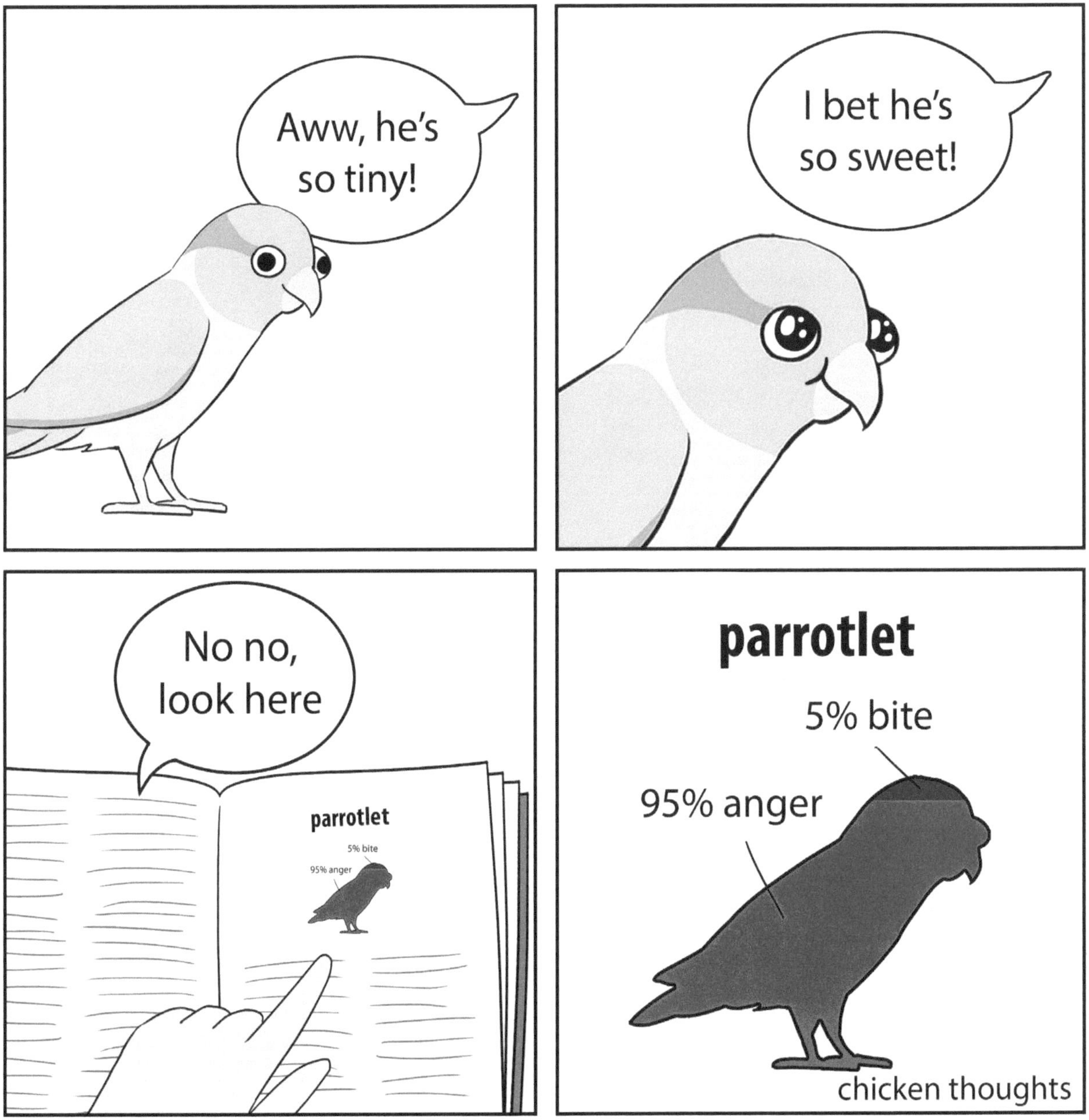
Aww, he's so tiny!
I bet he's so sweet!
No no, look here
parrotlet
5% bite
95% anger
parrotlet
5% bite
95% anger
chicken thoughts

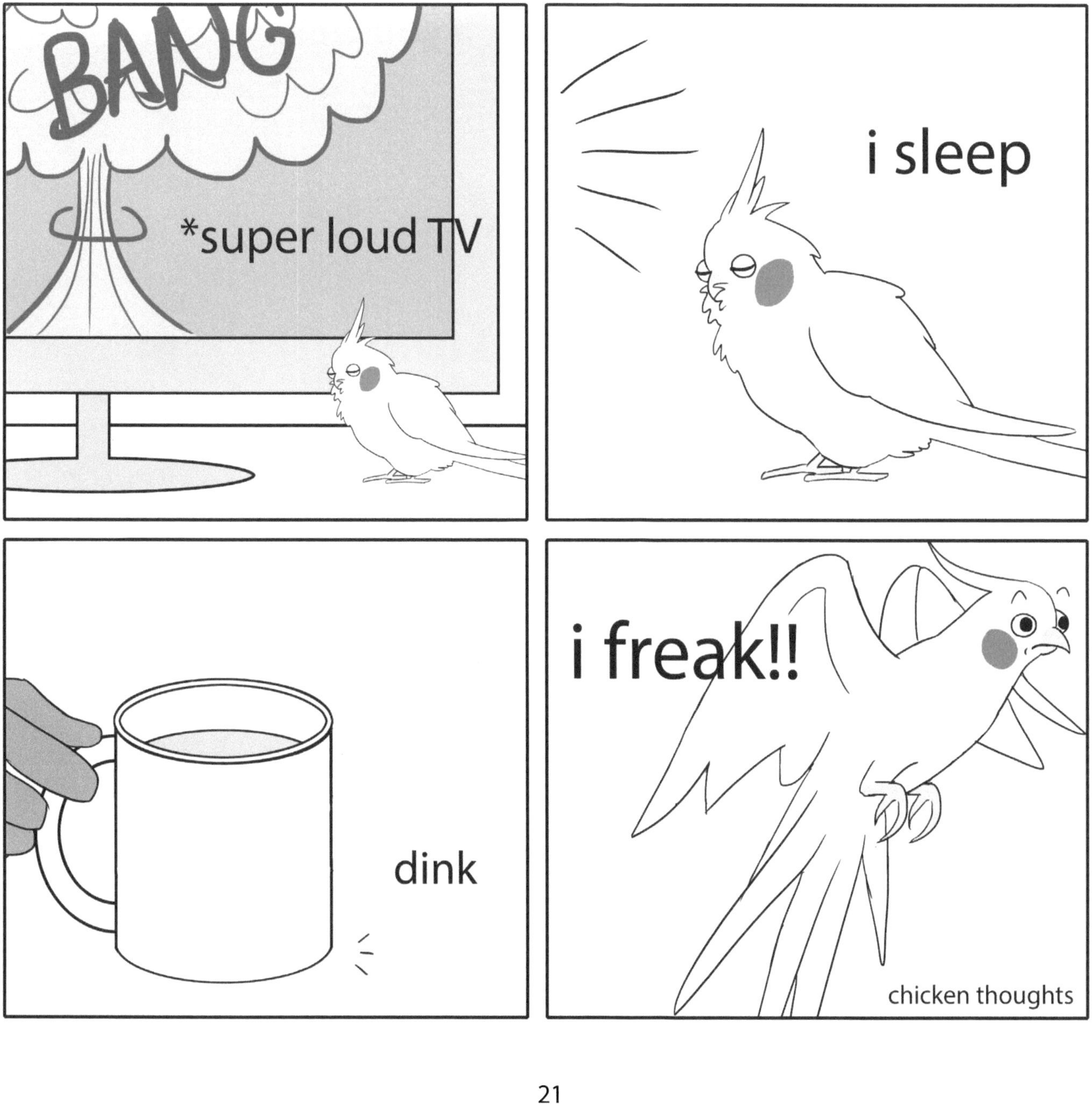
BANG
*super loud TV
i sleep
dink
i freak!!
chicken thoughts

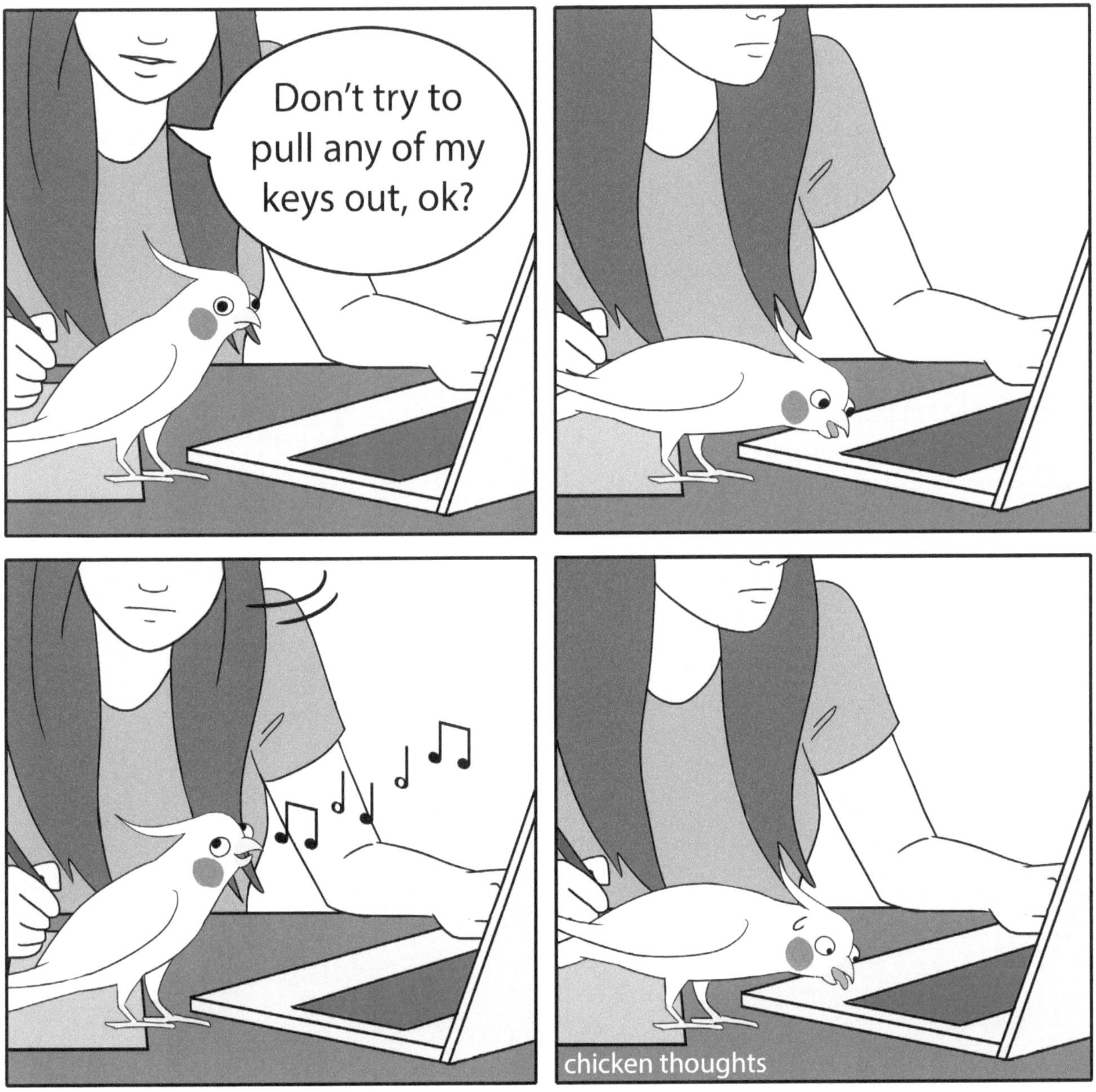
Don't try to pull any of my keys out, ok?
chicken thoughts

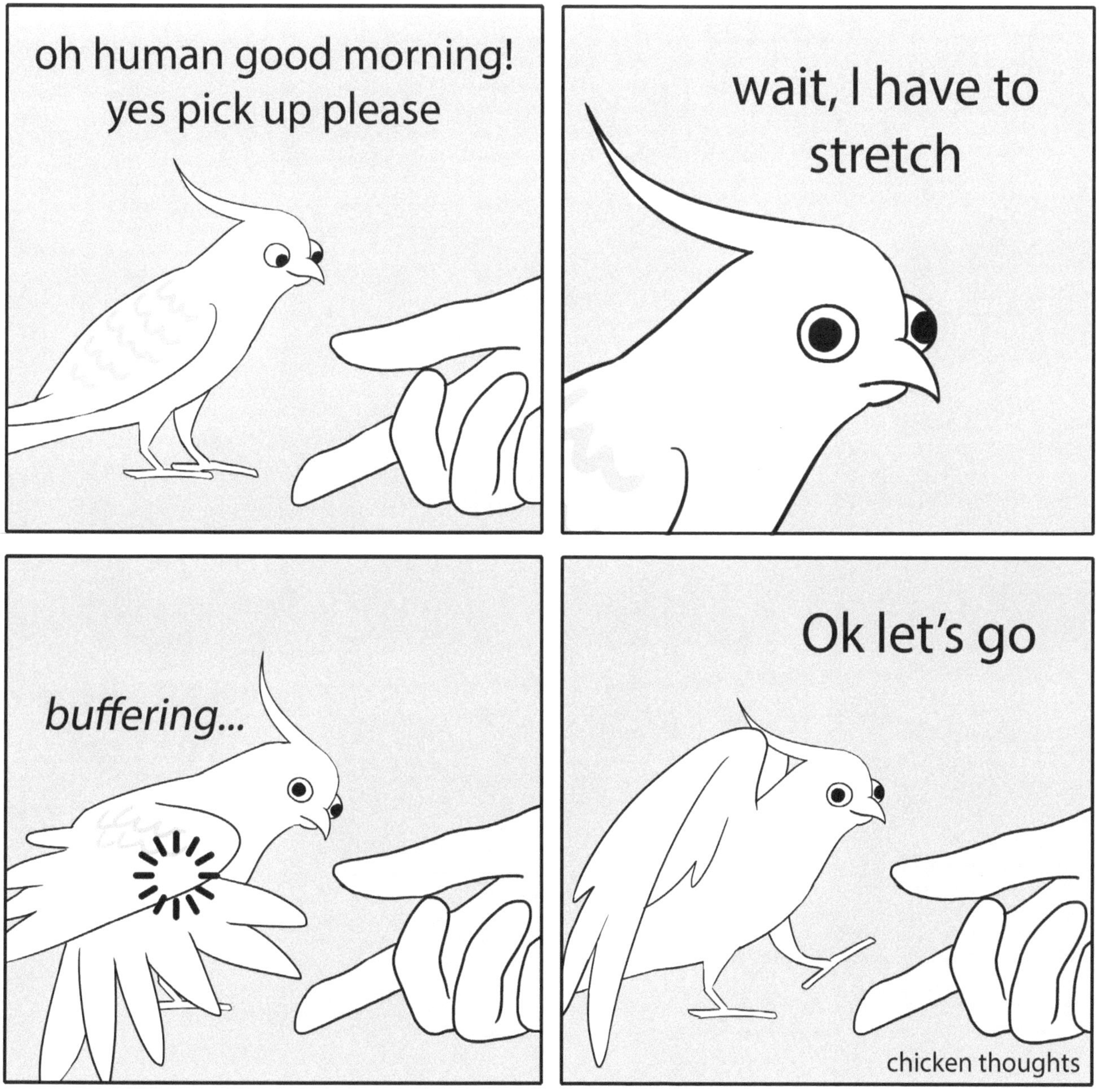
oh human good morning!
yes pick up please
wait, I have to
stretch
buffering...
Ok let's go
chicken thoughts

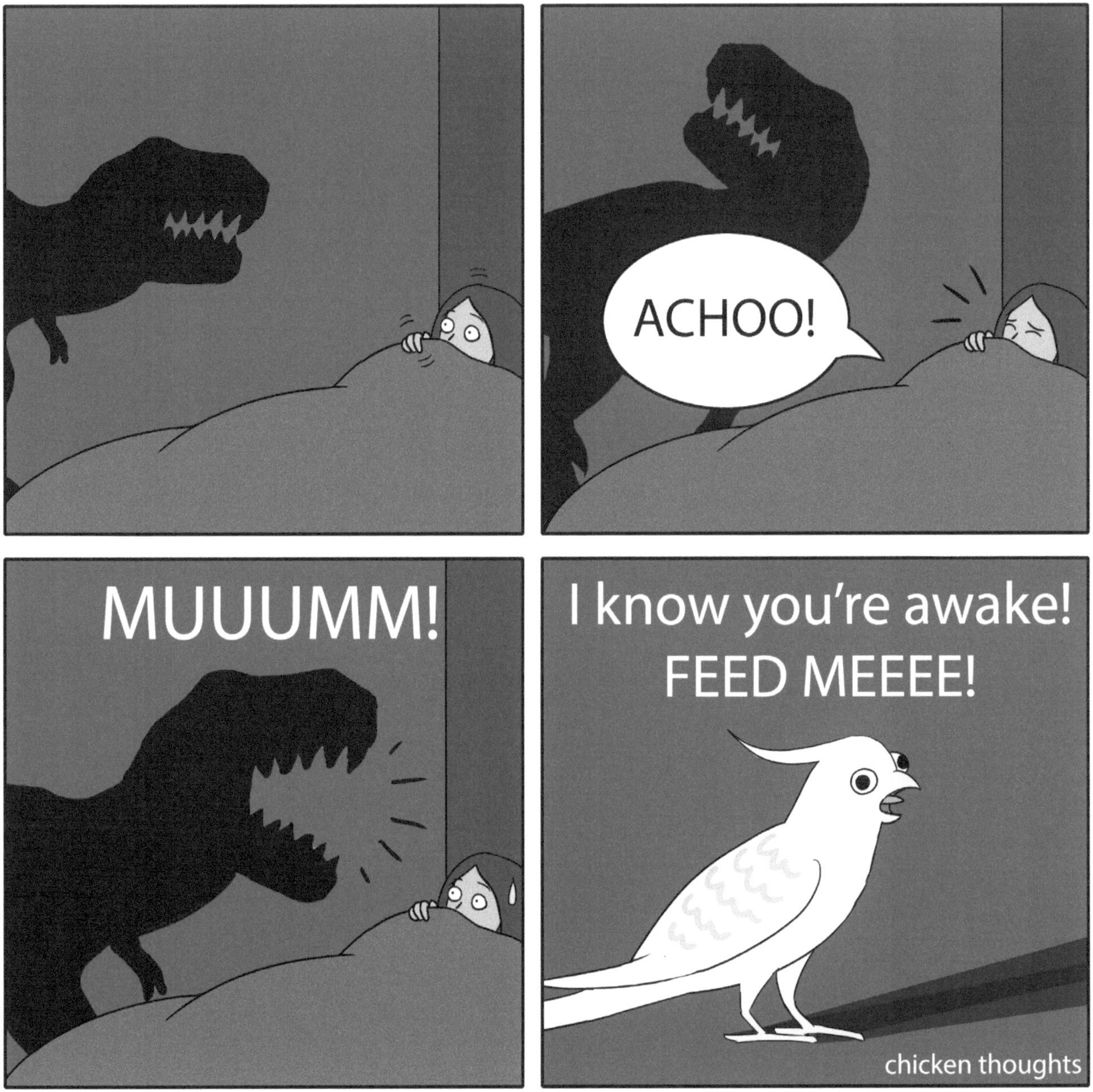
ACHOO!
MUUUMM!
I know you're awake!
FEED MEEEE!
chicken thoughts

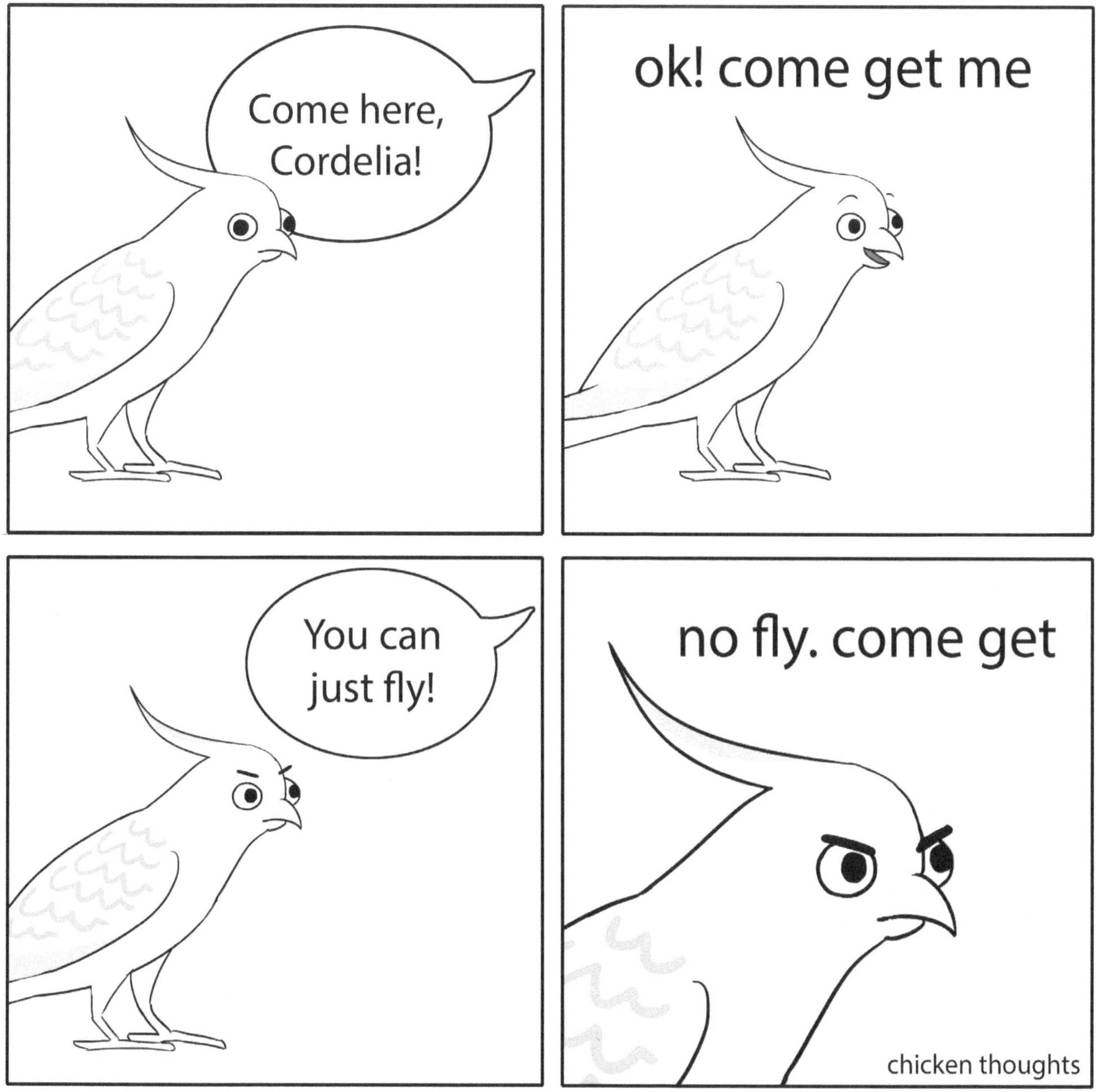
Come here, Cordelia!
ok! come get me
You can just fly!
no fly. come get
chicken thoughts

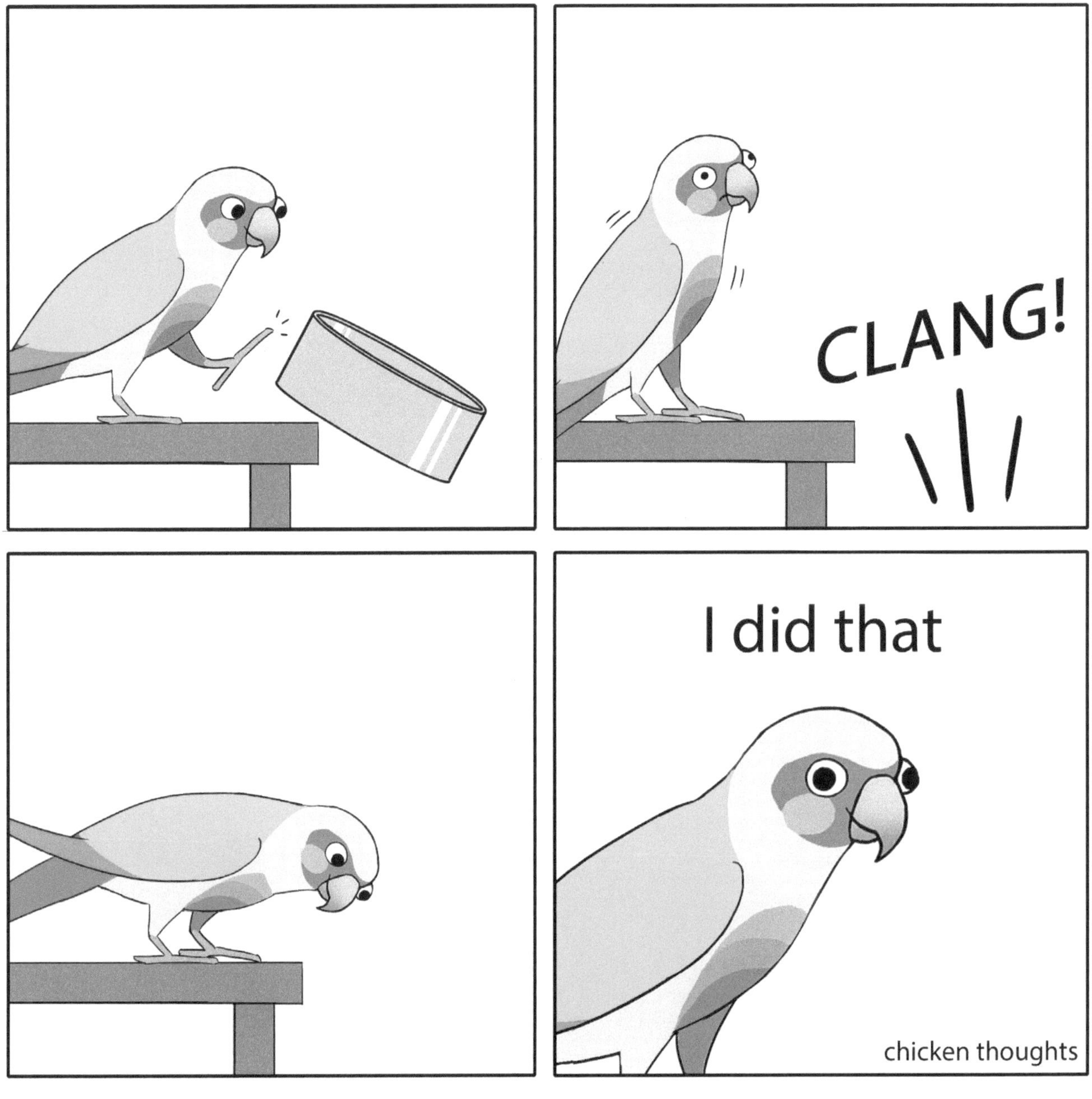
CLANG!
I did that
chicken thoughts

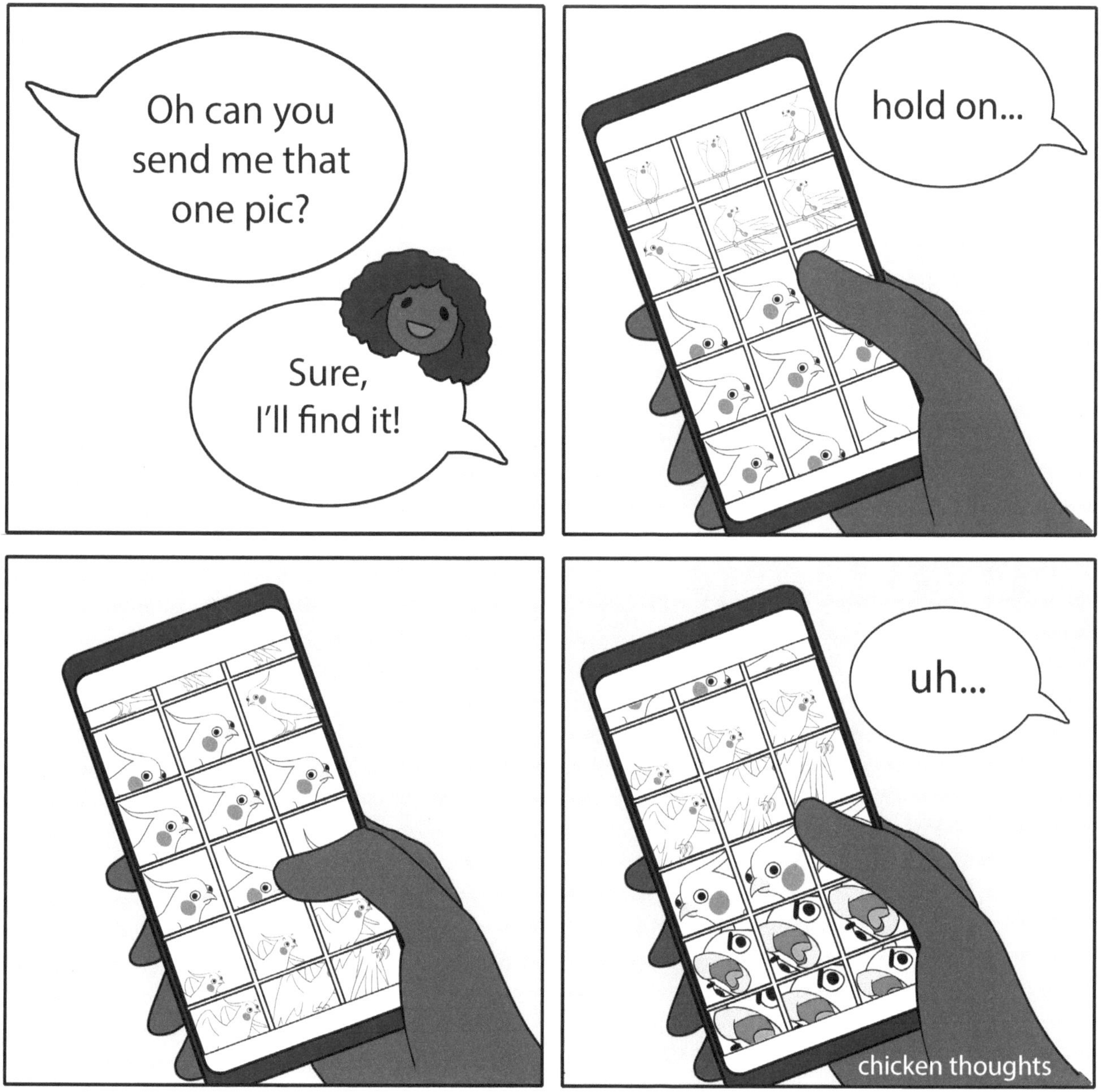
Oh can you send me that one pic?
Sure, I'll find it!
hold on...
uh...
chicken thoughts

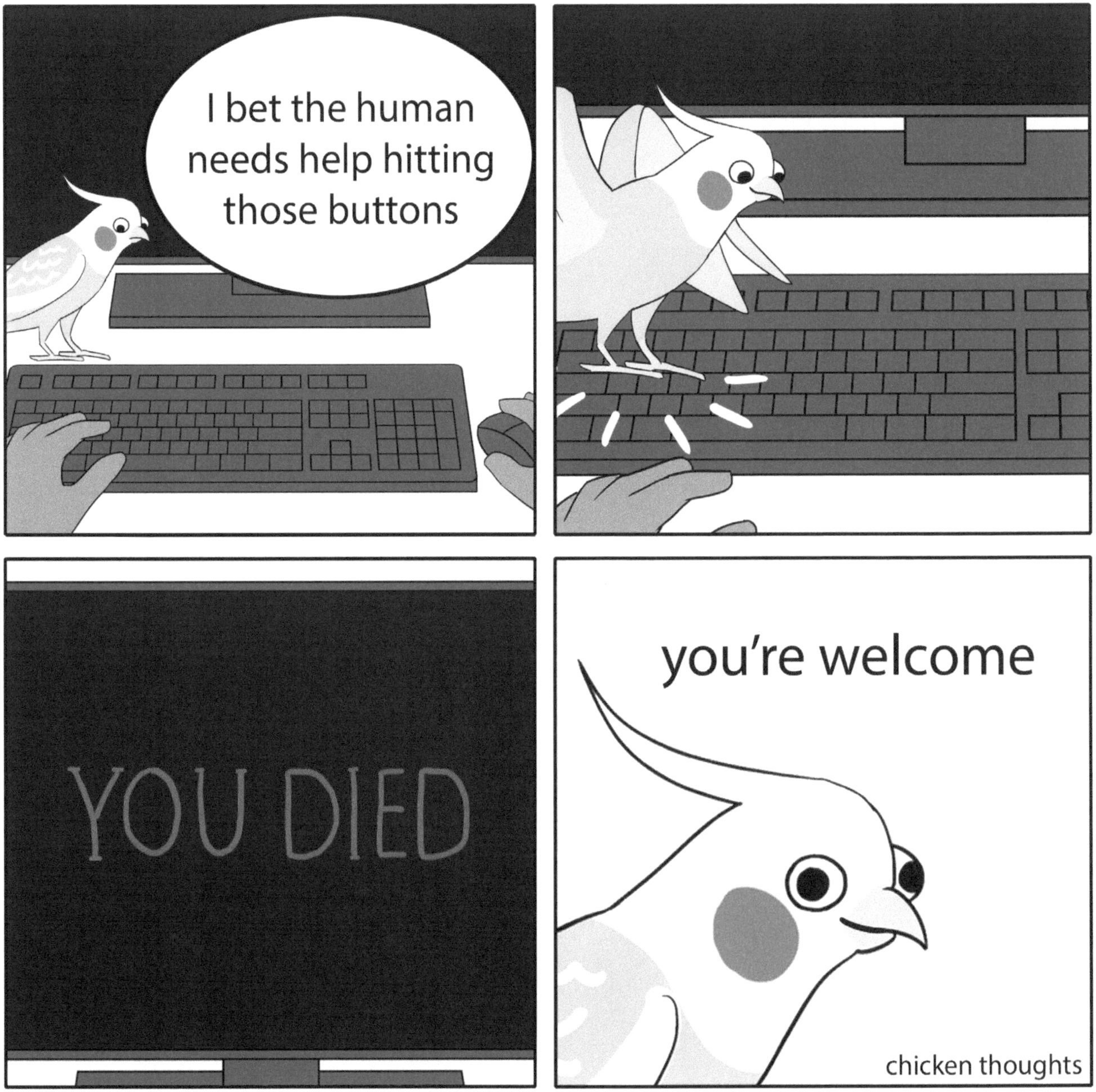
I bet the human needs help hitting those buttons
YOU DIED
you're welcome
chicken thoughts

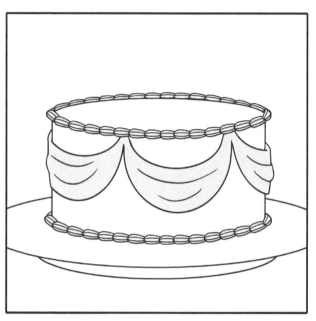

I helped

chicken thoughts

29

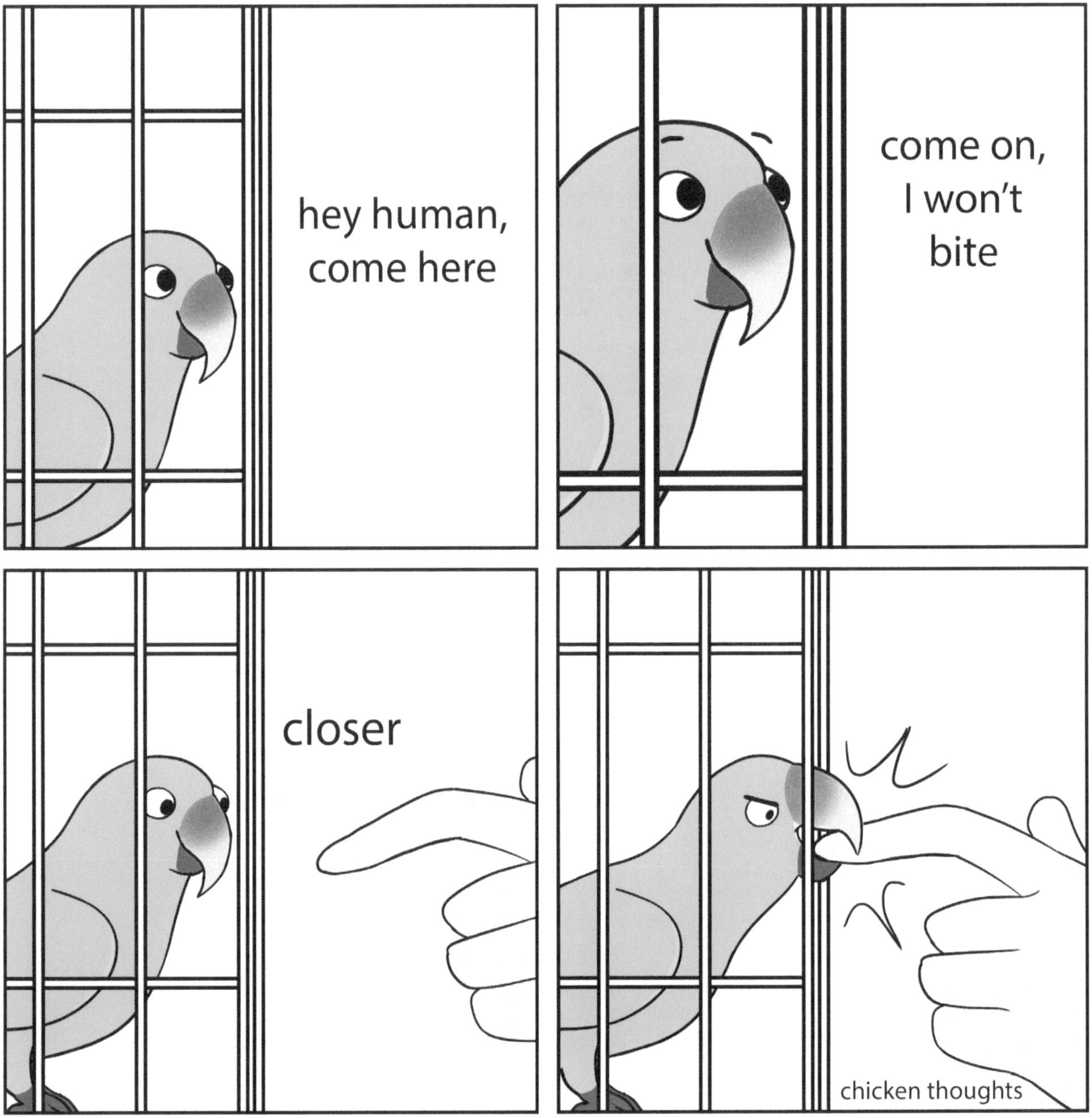
hey human, come here
come on, I won't bite
closer
chicken thoughts

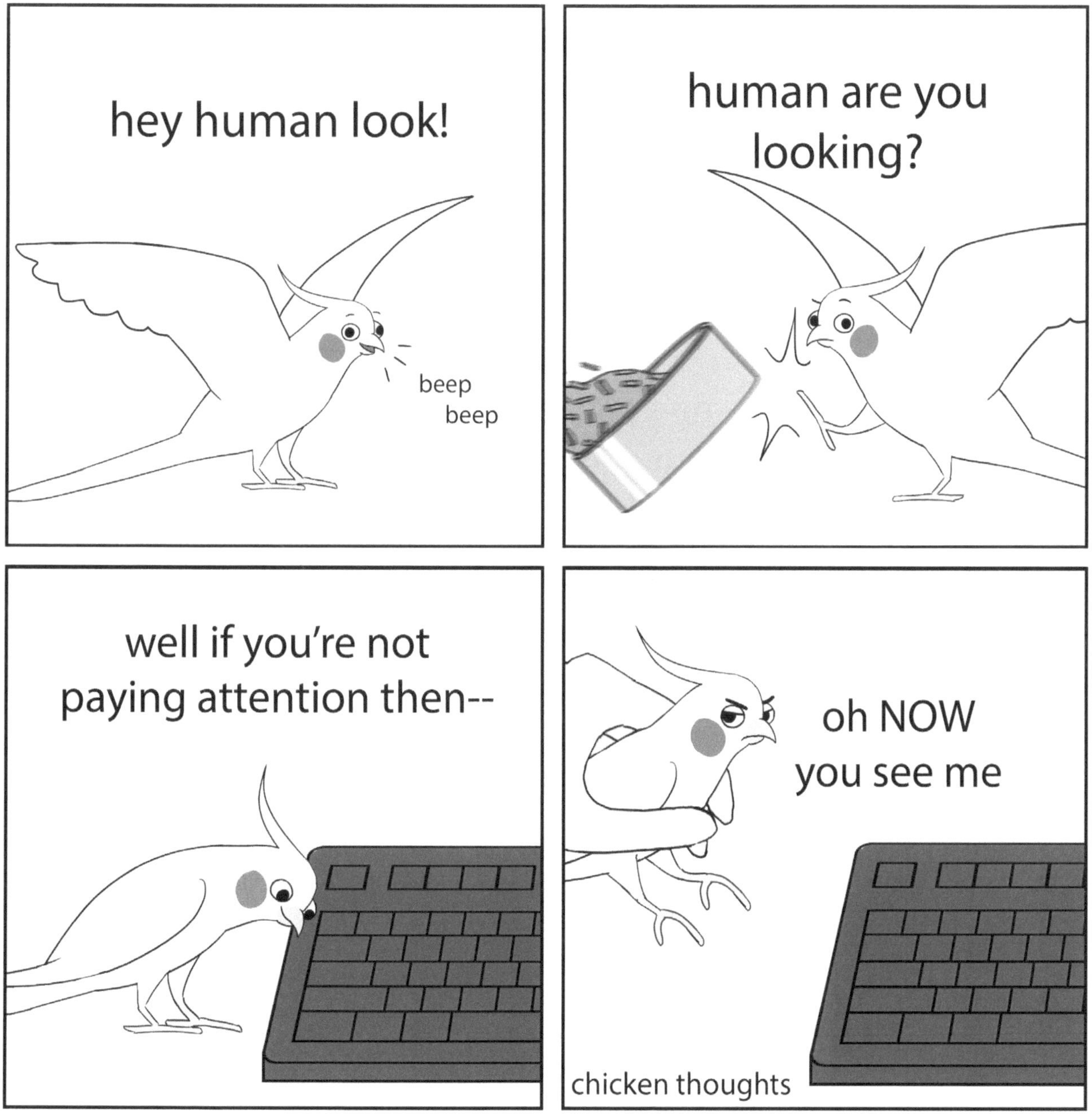
hey human look!
beep
beep
human are you looking?
well if you're not paying attention then--
oh NOW you see me
chicken thoughts

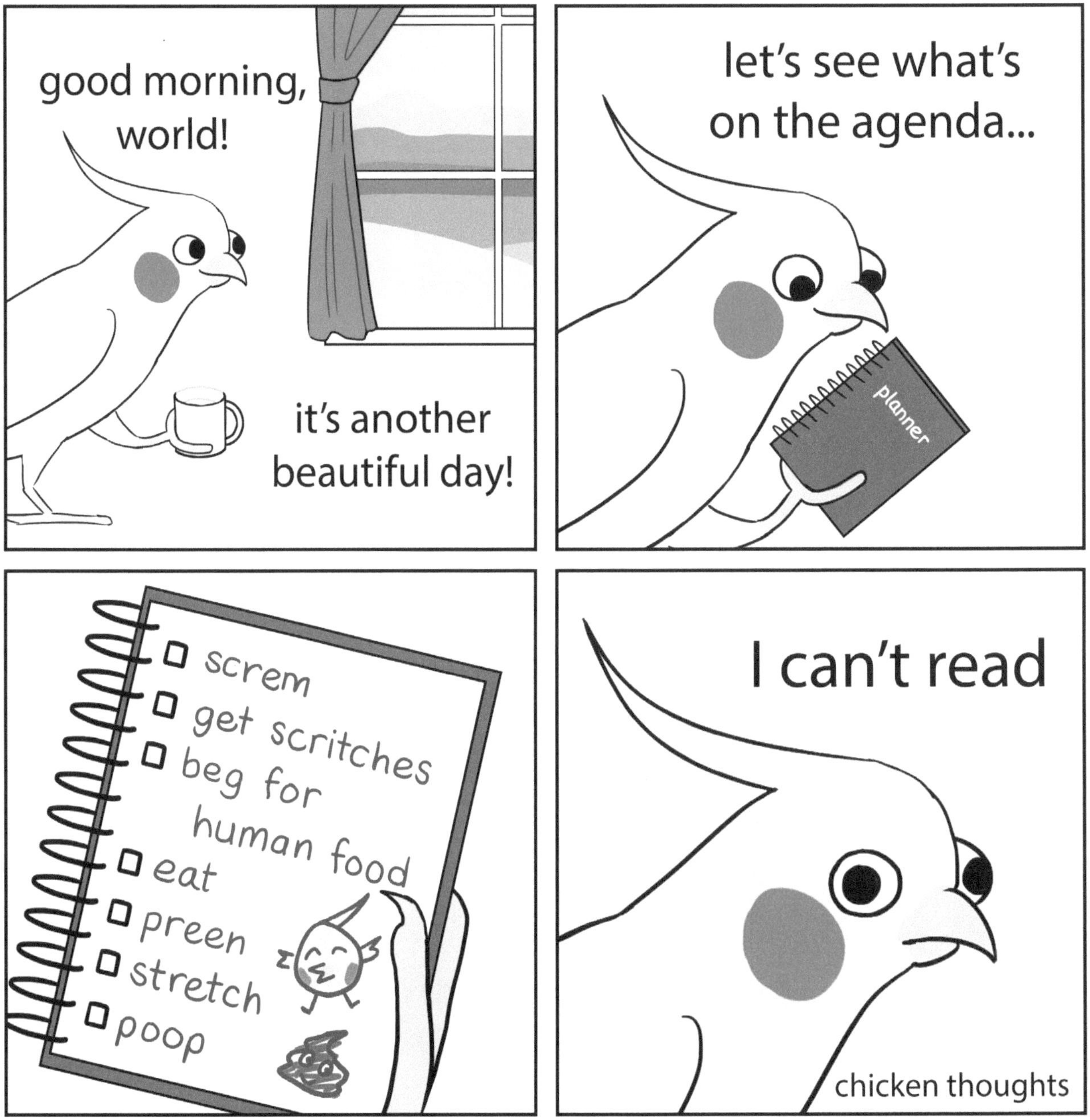
good morning, world!
it's another beautiful day!
let's see what's on the agenda...
planner
screm
get scritches
beg for human food
eat
preen
stretch
poop
I can't read
chicken thoughts

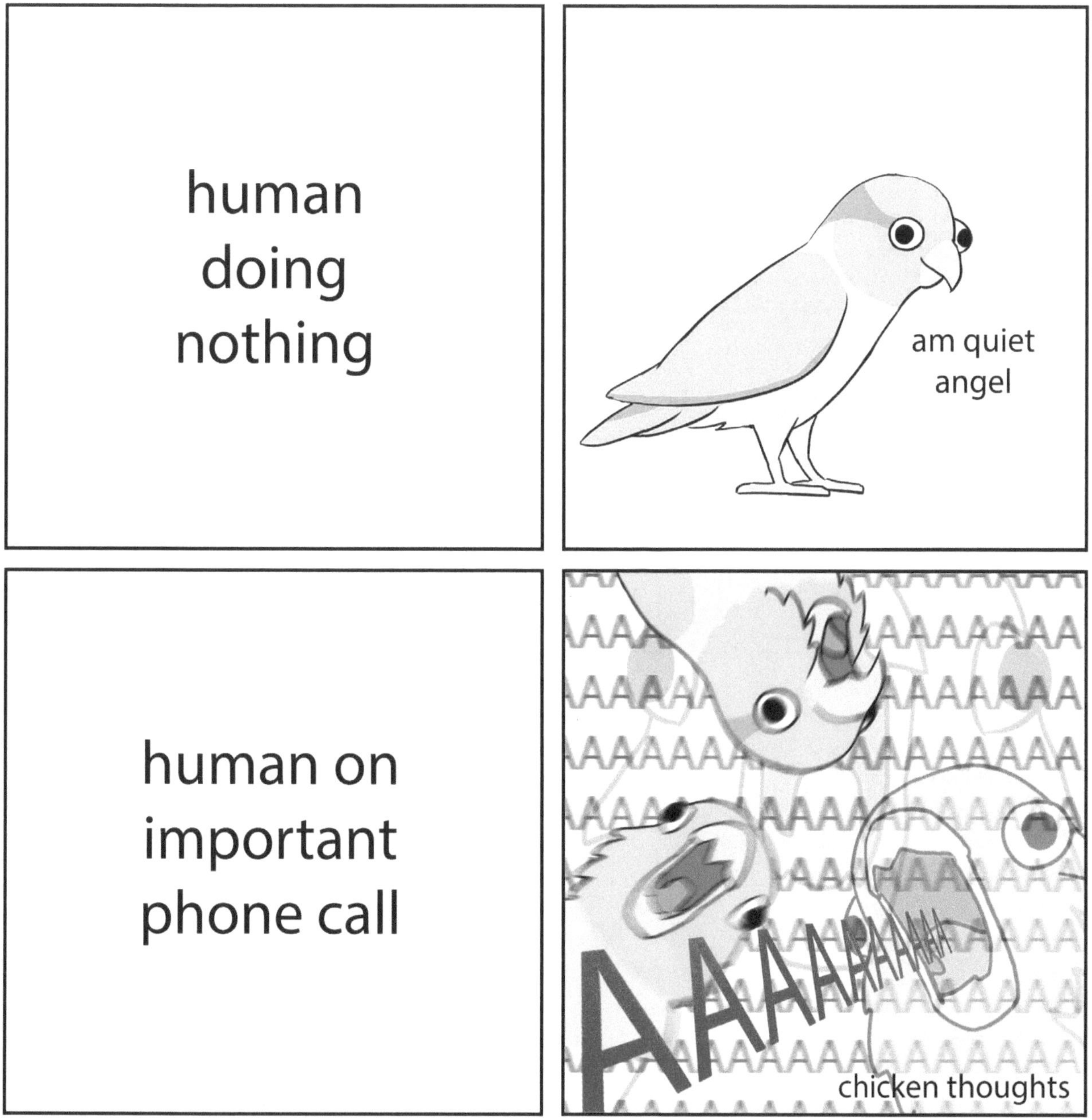
human doing nothing
am quiet angel
human on important phone call
AAAAAAAAA
chicken thoughts

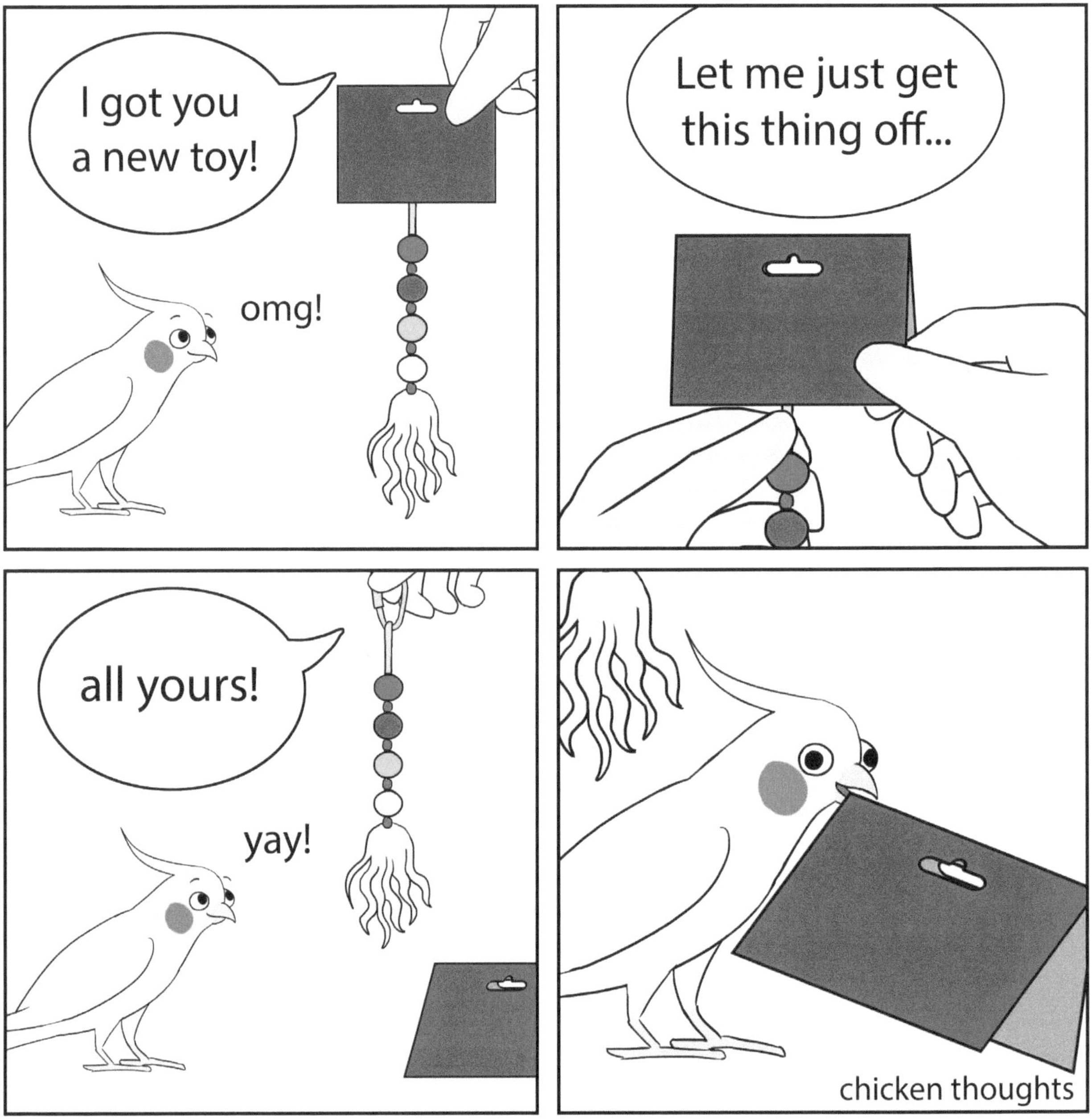
I got you a new toy!
omg!
Let me just get this thing off...
all yours!
yay!
chicken thoughts

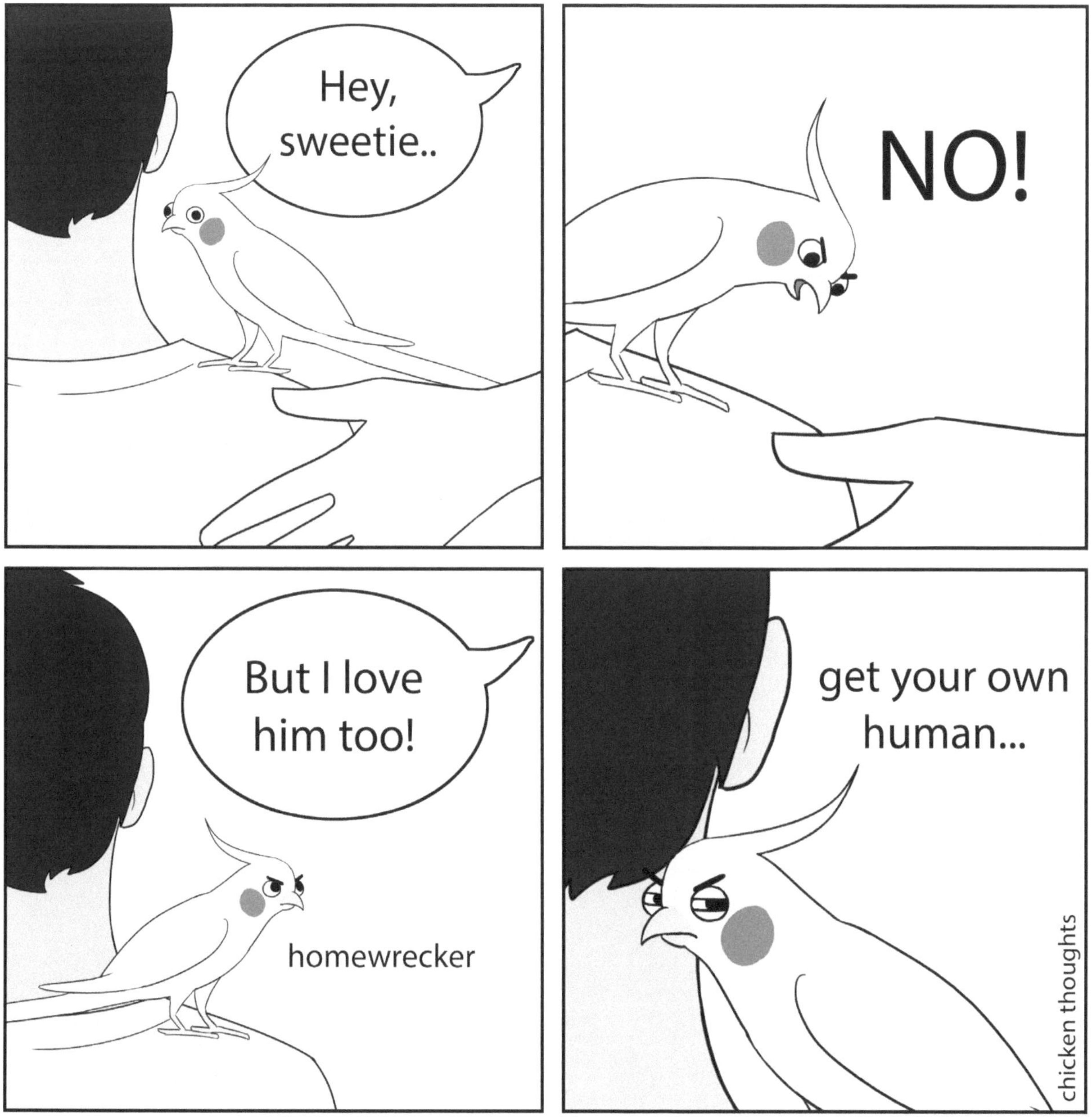
Hey, sweetie..
NO!
But I love him too!
homewrecker
get your own human...
chicken thoughts

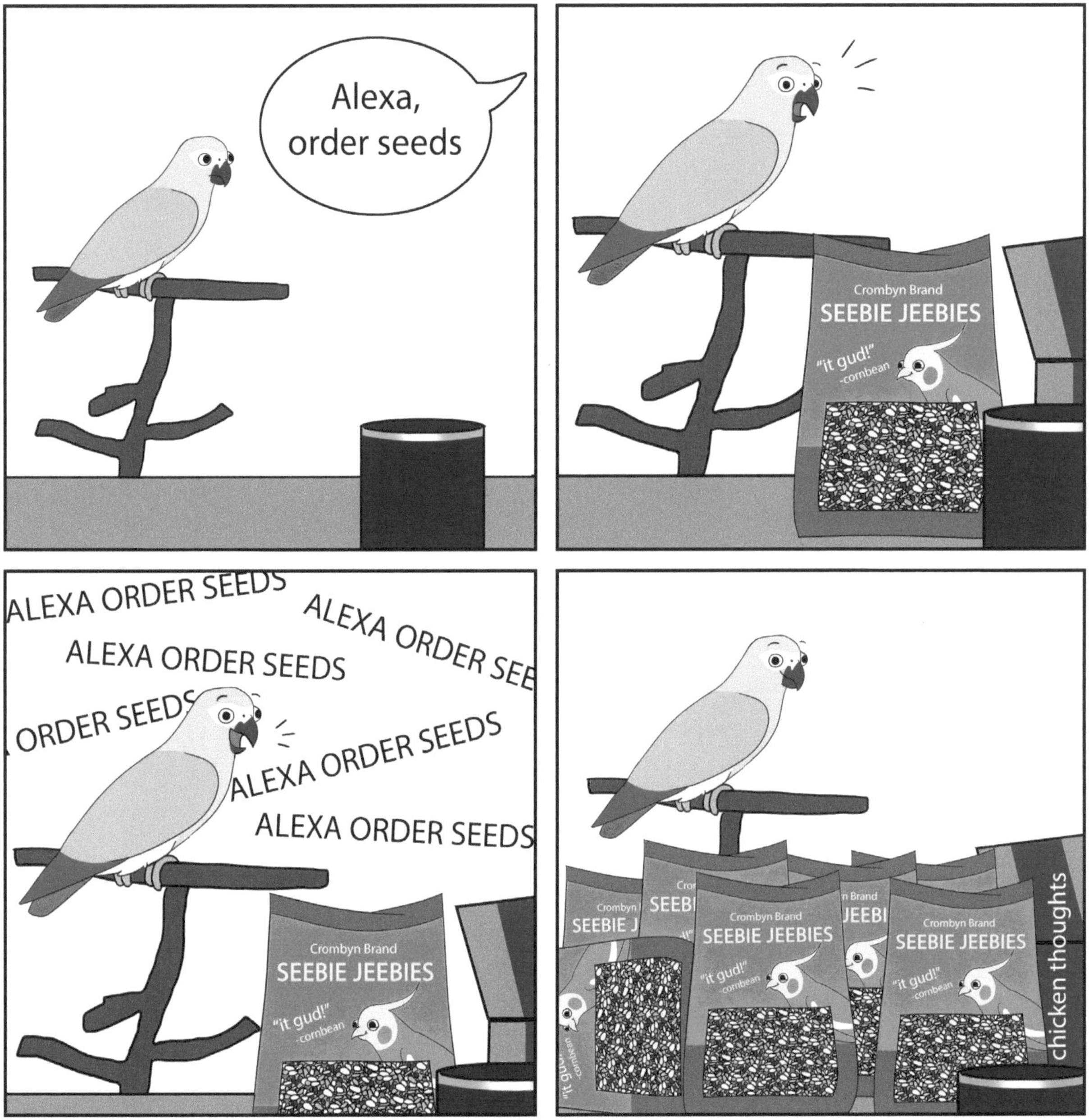
Alexa,
order seeds
Crombyn Brand
SEEBIE JEEBIES
"it gud!"
-cornbean
ALEXA ORDER SEEDS
ALEXA ORDER SEEDS
ALEXA ORDER SEEDS
ALEXA ORDER SEEDS
chicken thoughts

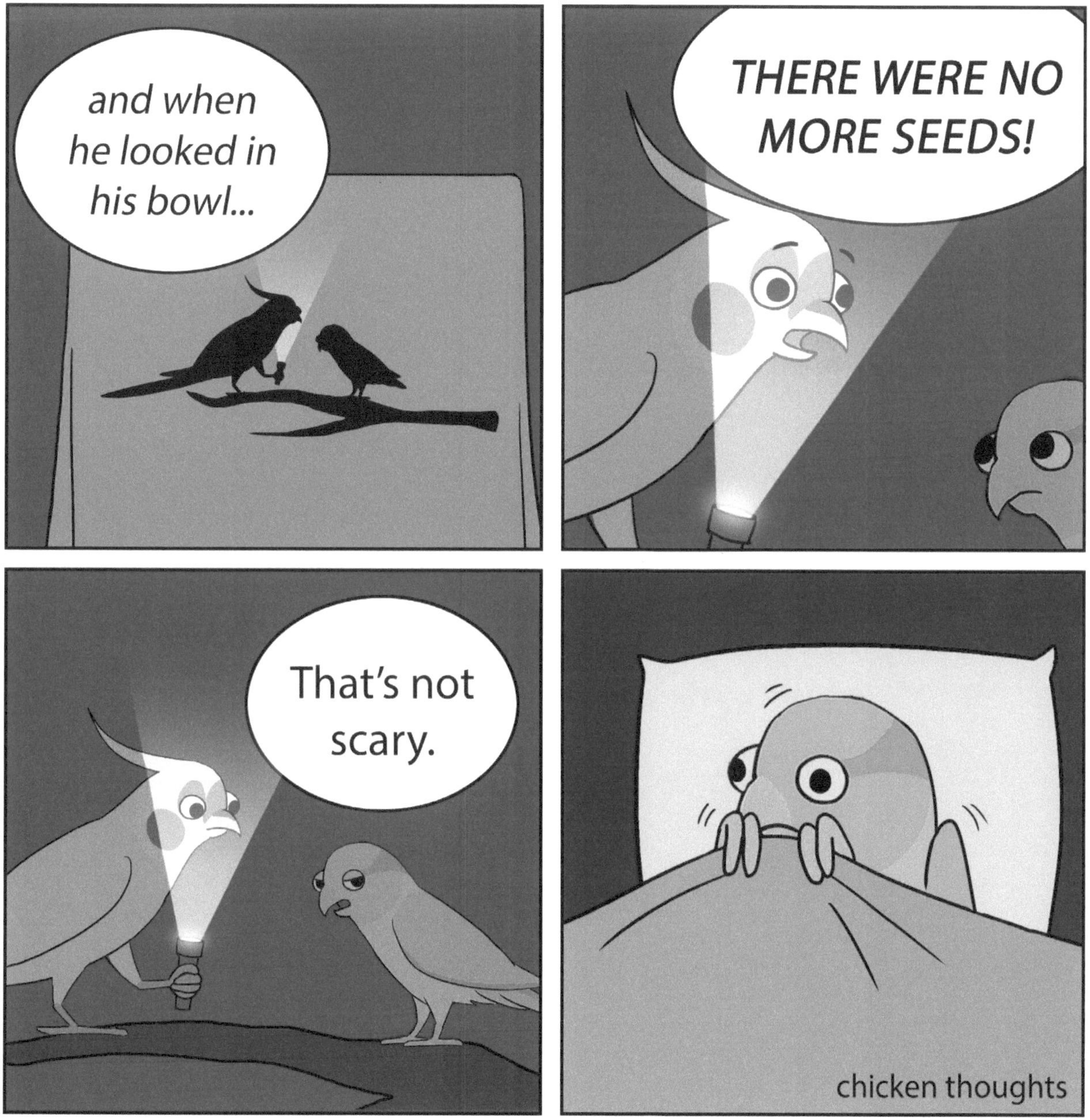
and when he looked in his bowl...
THERE WERE NO MORE SEEDS!
That's not scary.
chicken thoughts

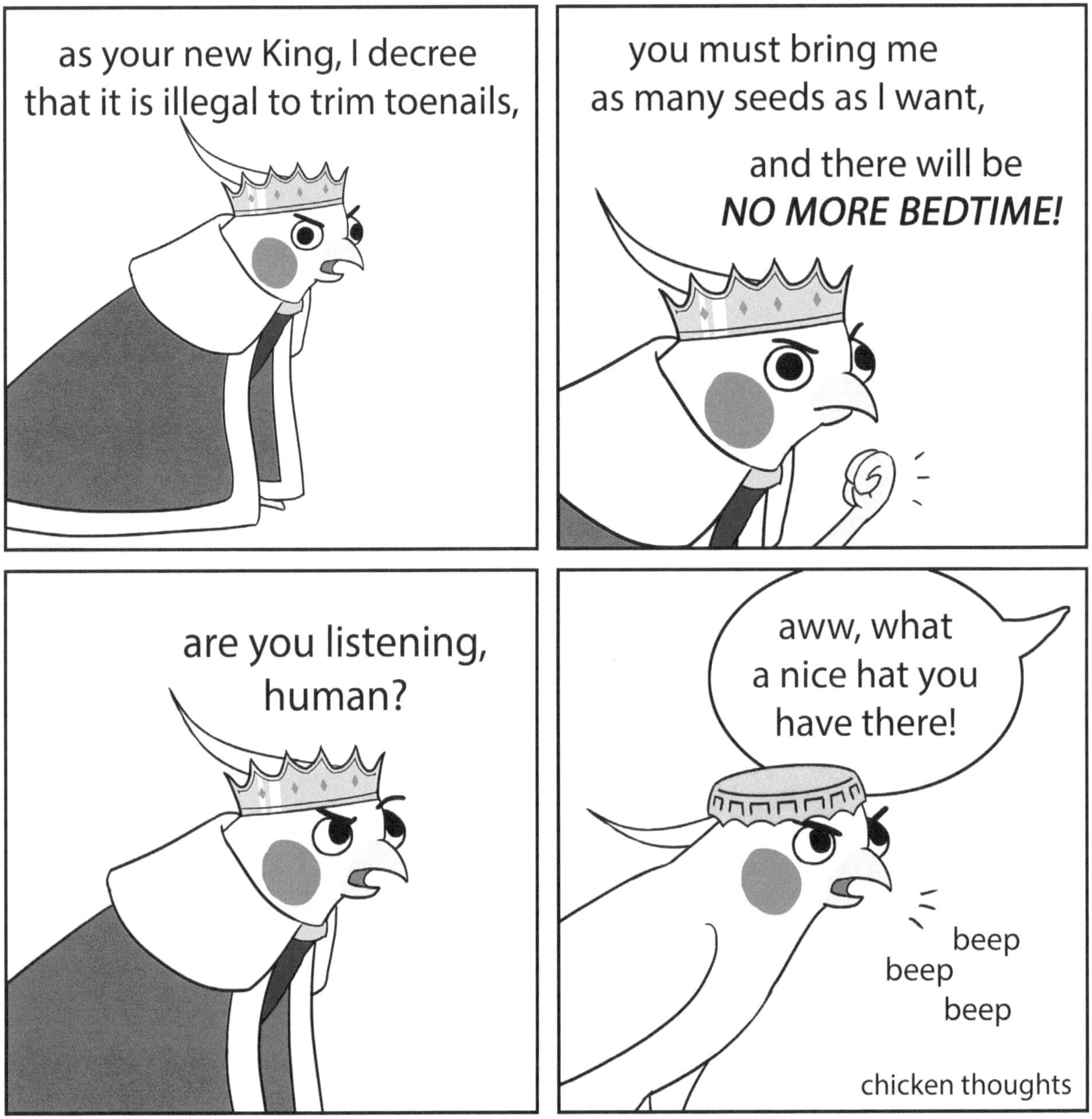
as your new King, I decree that it is illegal to trim toenails,
you must bring me as many seeds as I want,
and there will be *NO MORE BEDTIME!*
are you listening, human?
aww, what a nice hat you have there!
beep
beep
beep
chicken thoughts

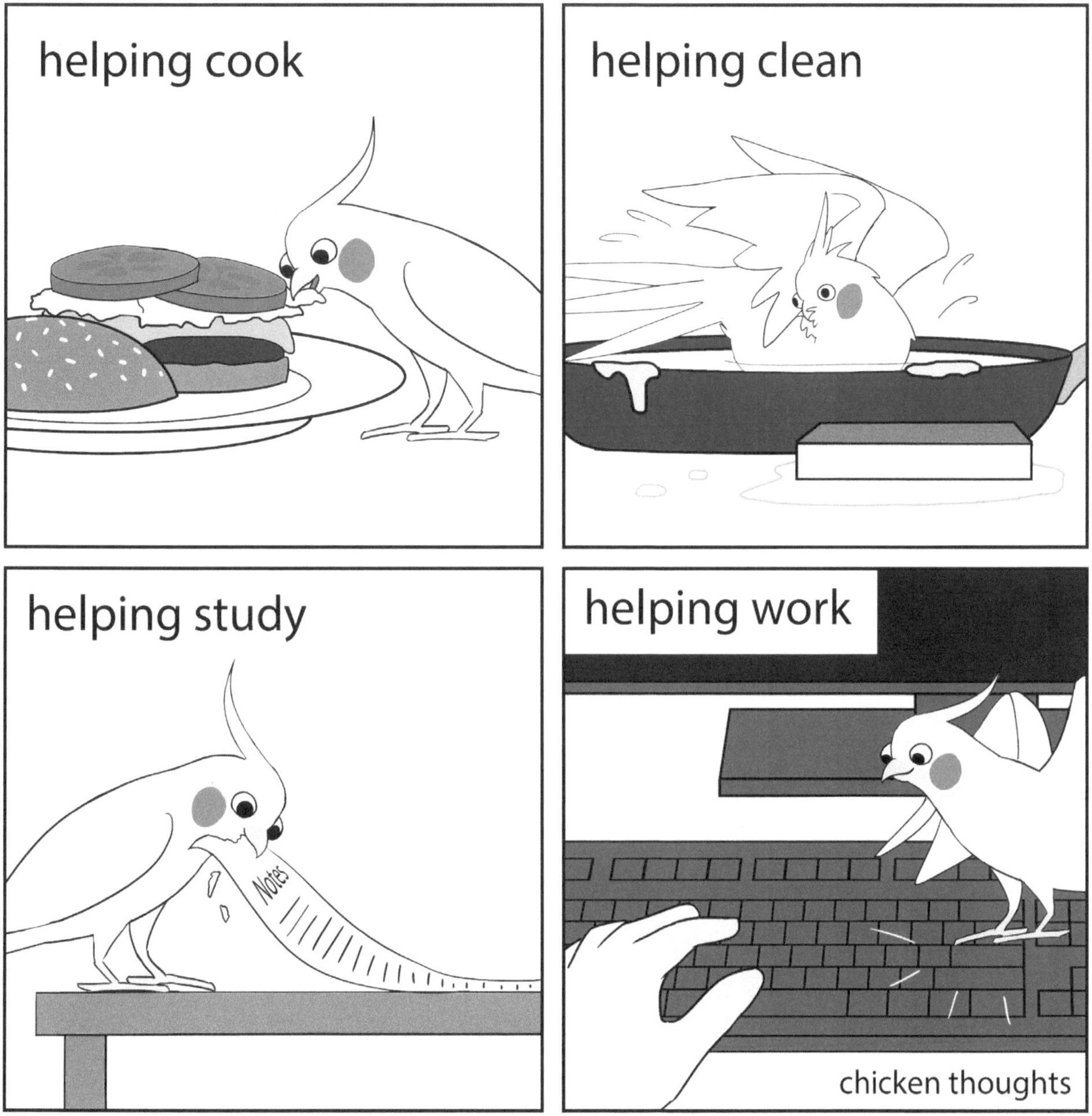
helping cook
helping clean
helping study
Notes
helping work
chicken thoughts

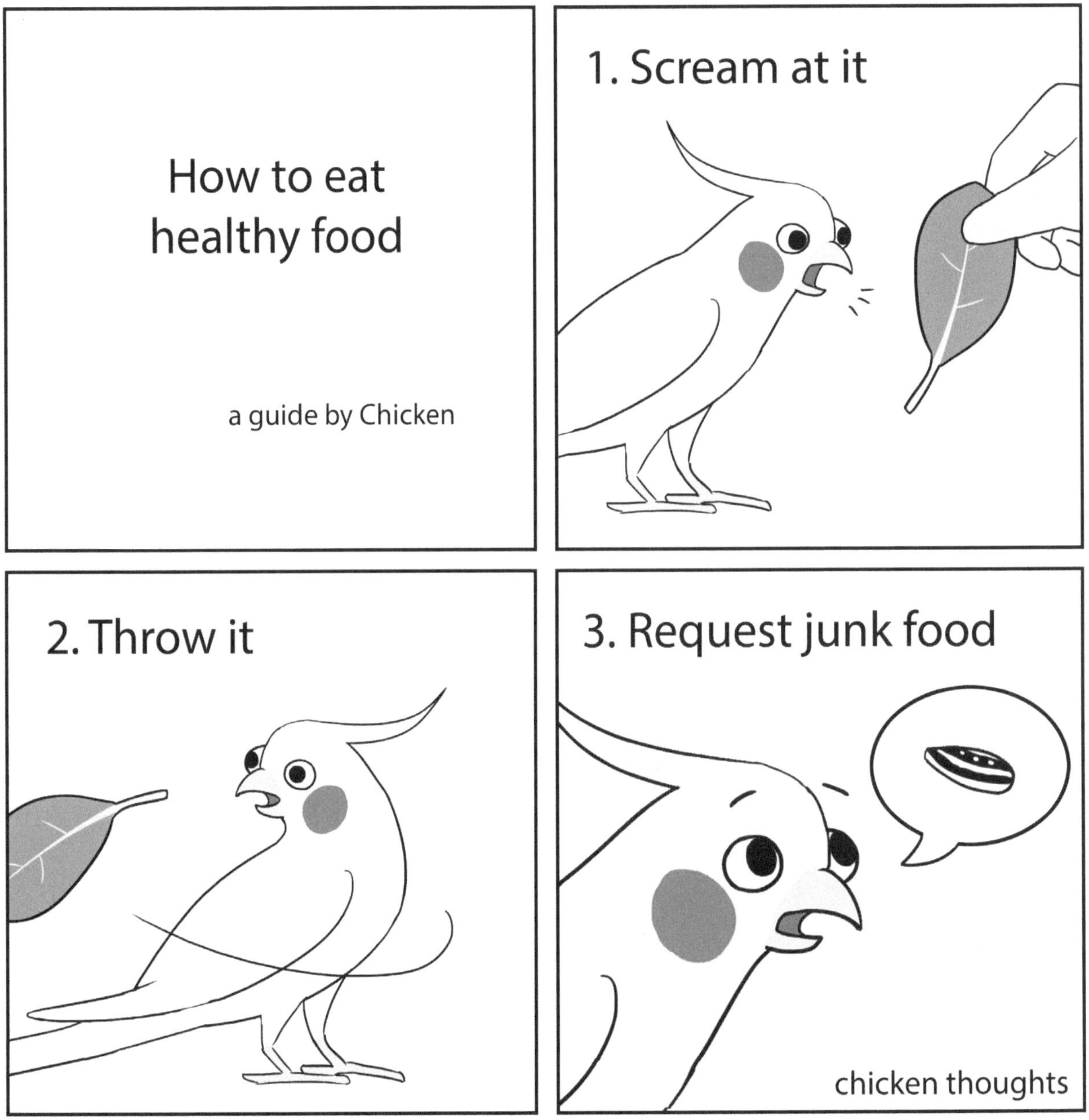
How to eat healthy food
a guide by Chicken
1. Scream at it
2. Throw it
3. Request junk food
chicken thoughts

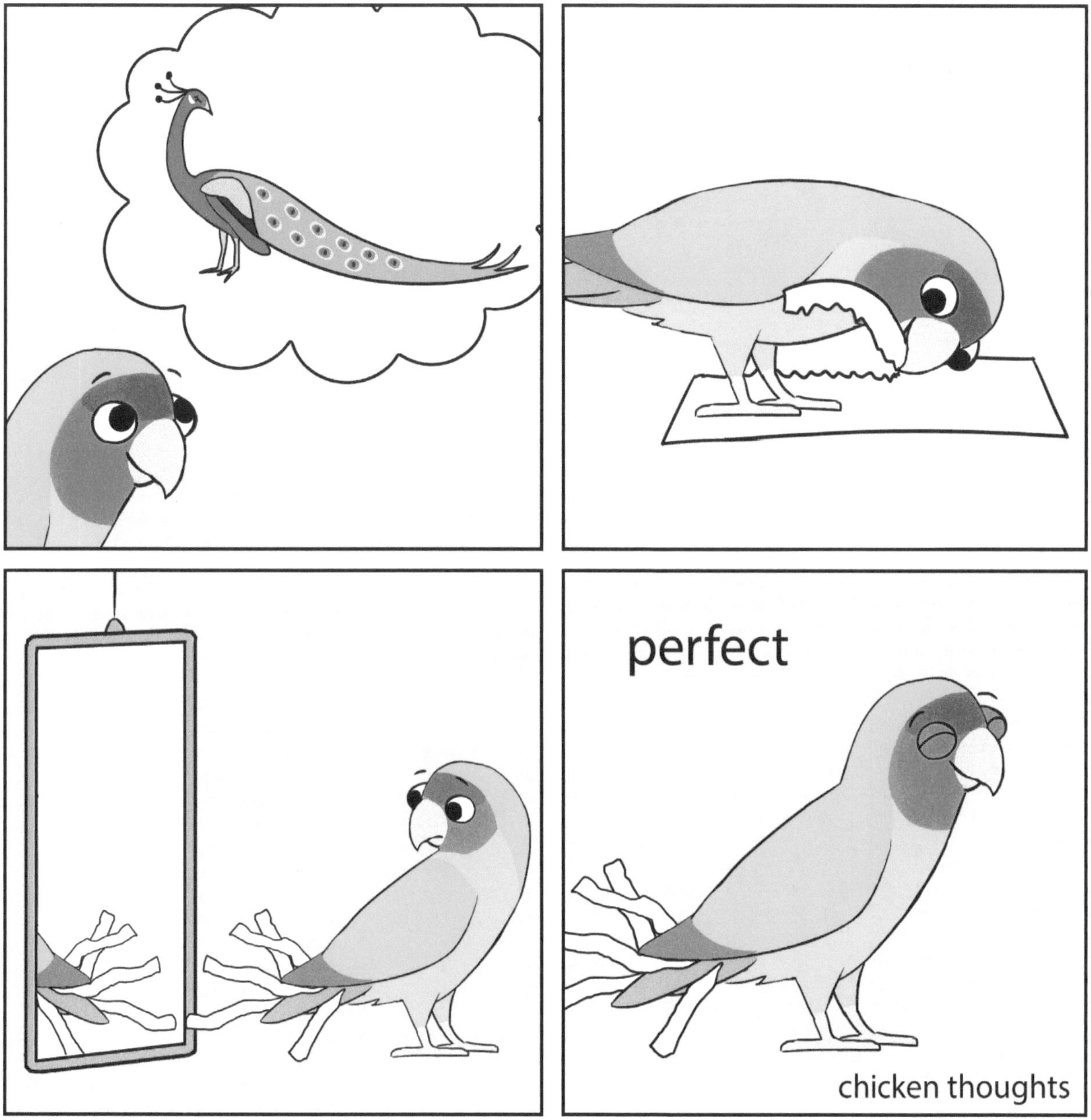
perfect
chicken thoughts

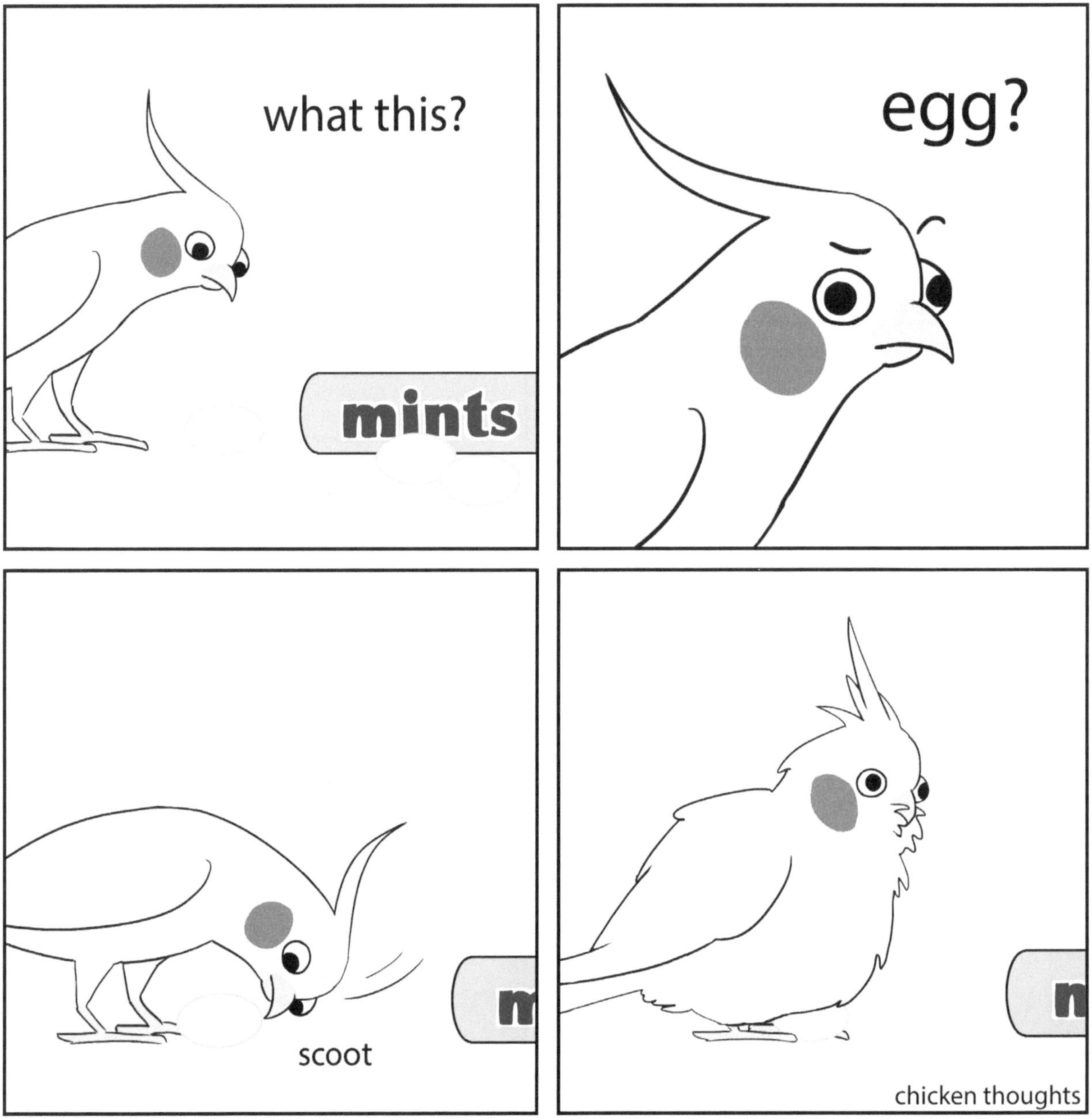
what this?
mints
egg?
scoot
chicken thoughts

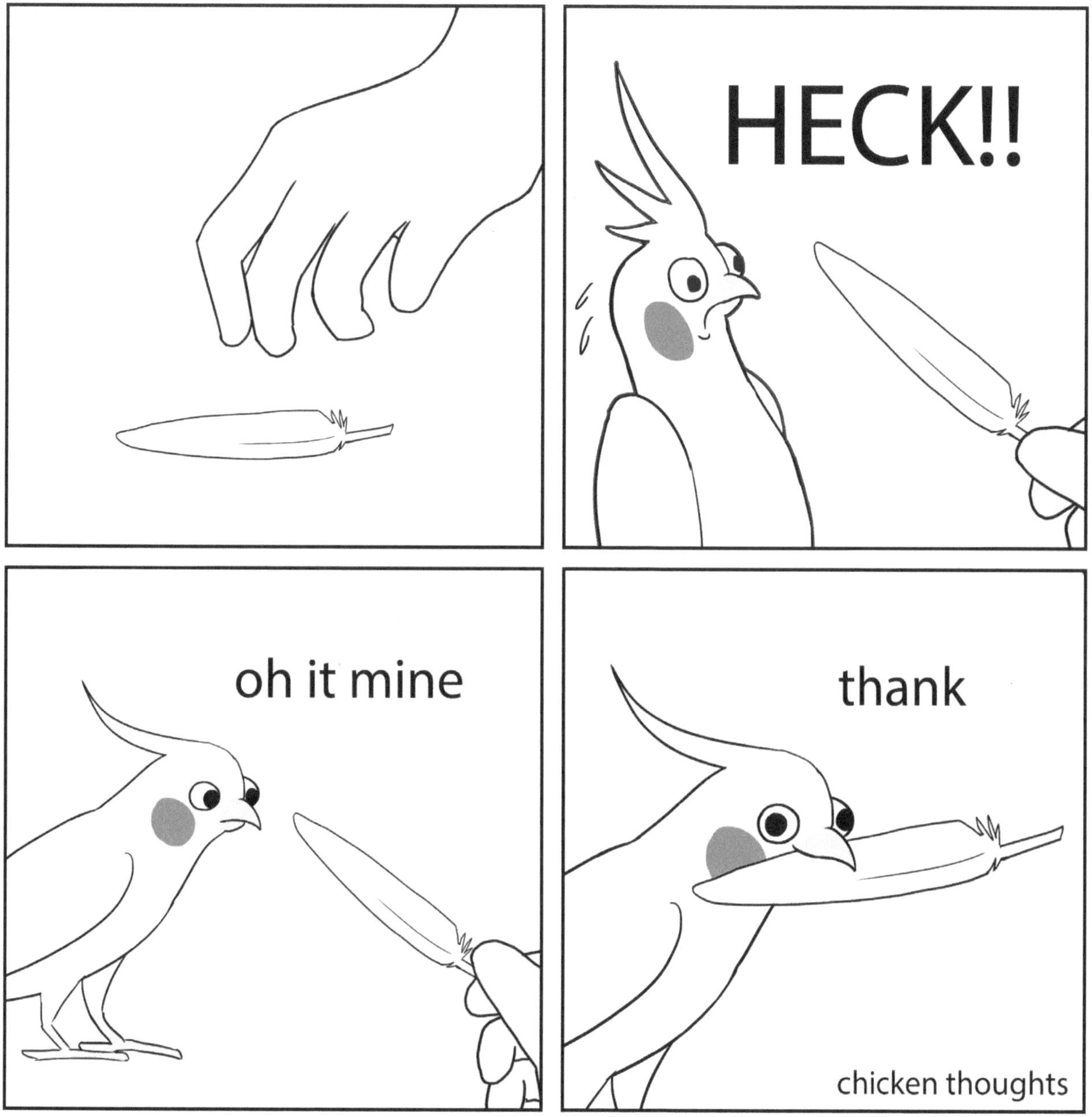
HECK!!
oh it mine
thank
chicken thoughts

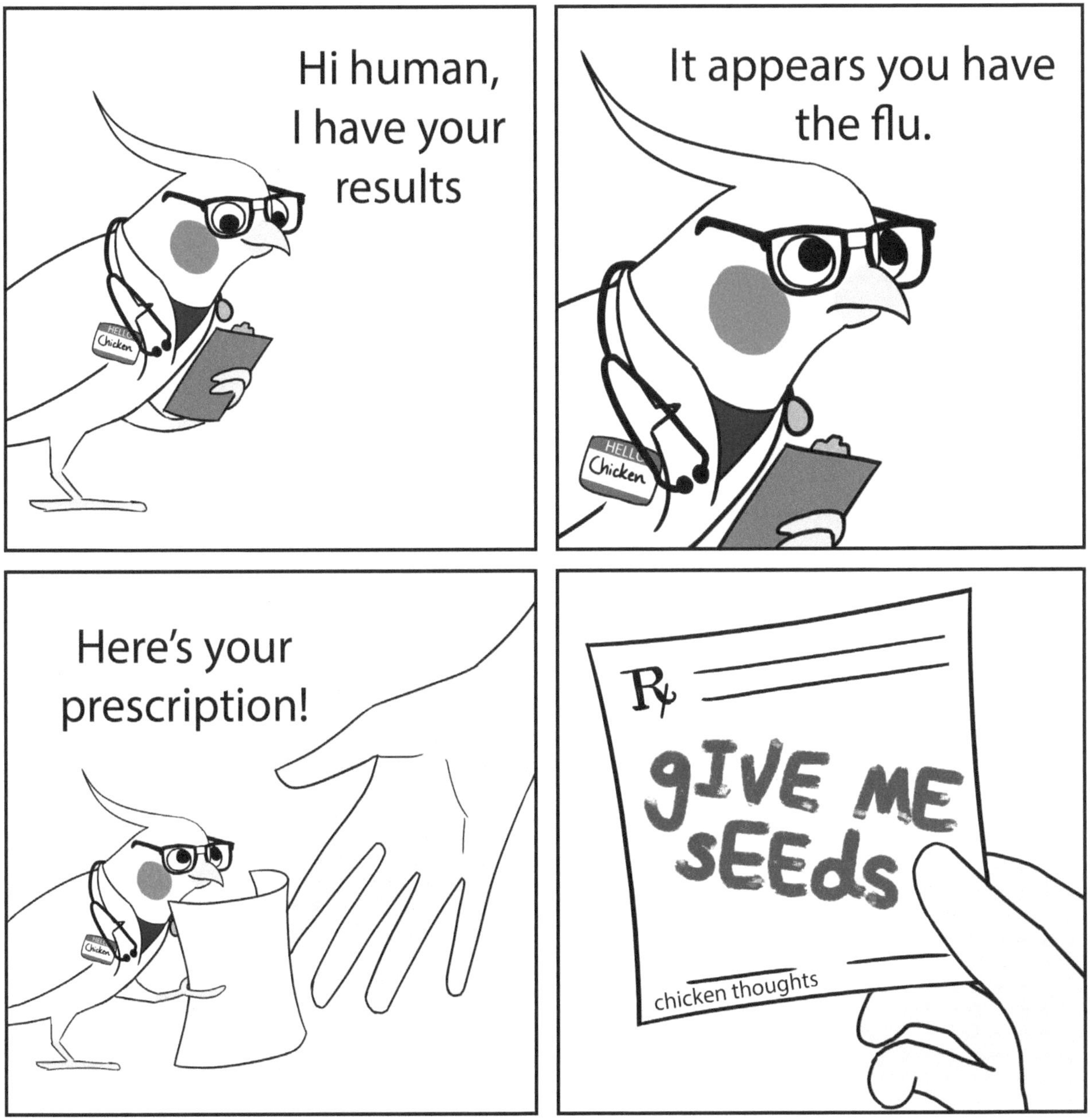
Hi human,
I have your
results
It appears you have
the flu.
HELLO
Chicken
Here's your
prescription!
℞
gIVE ME
SEEds
chicken thoughts

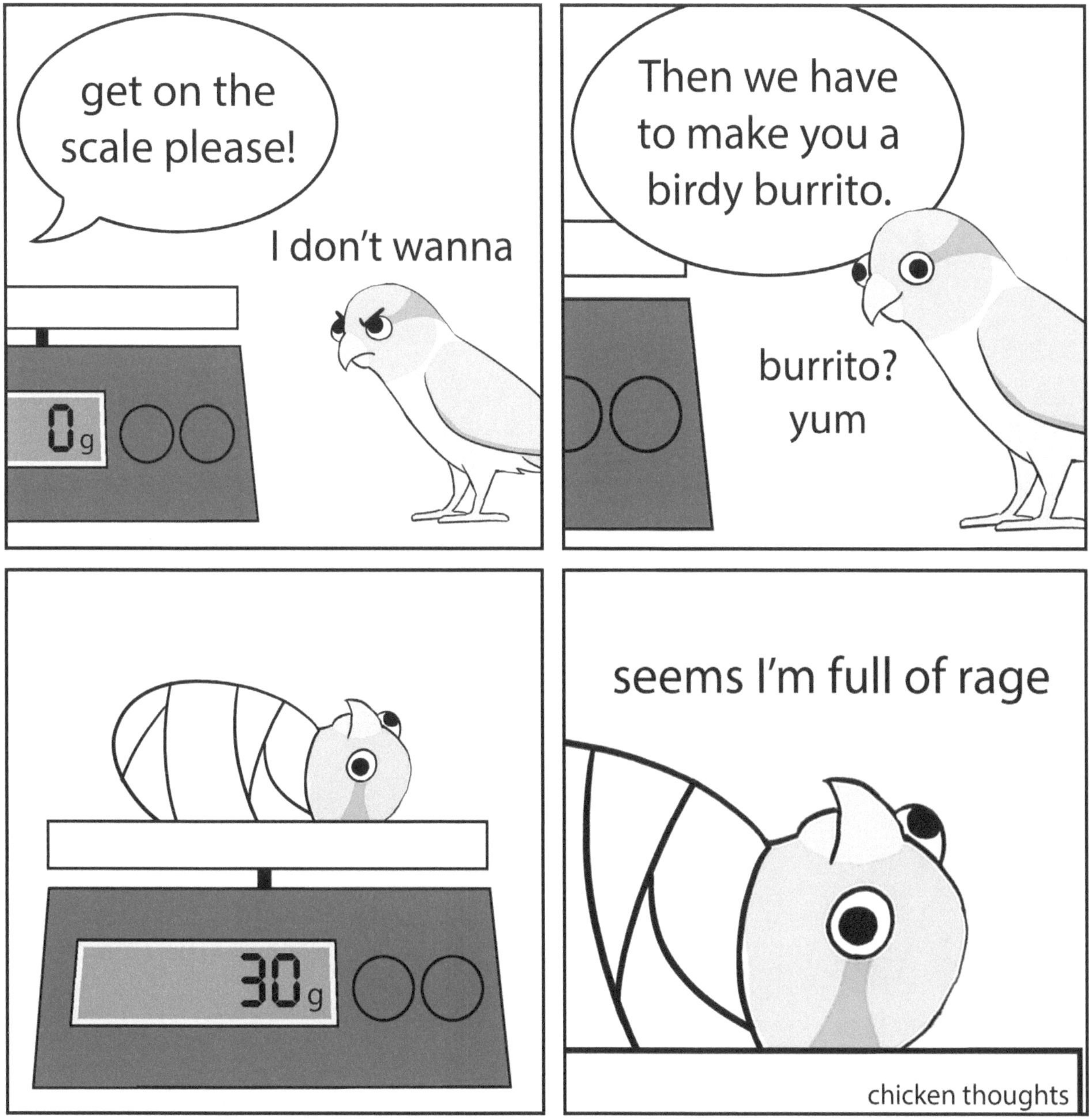
get on the scale please!
I don't wanna
0g
Then we have to make you a birdy burrito.
burrito? yum
30g
seems I'm full of rage
chicken thoughts

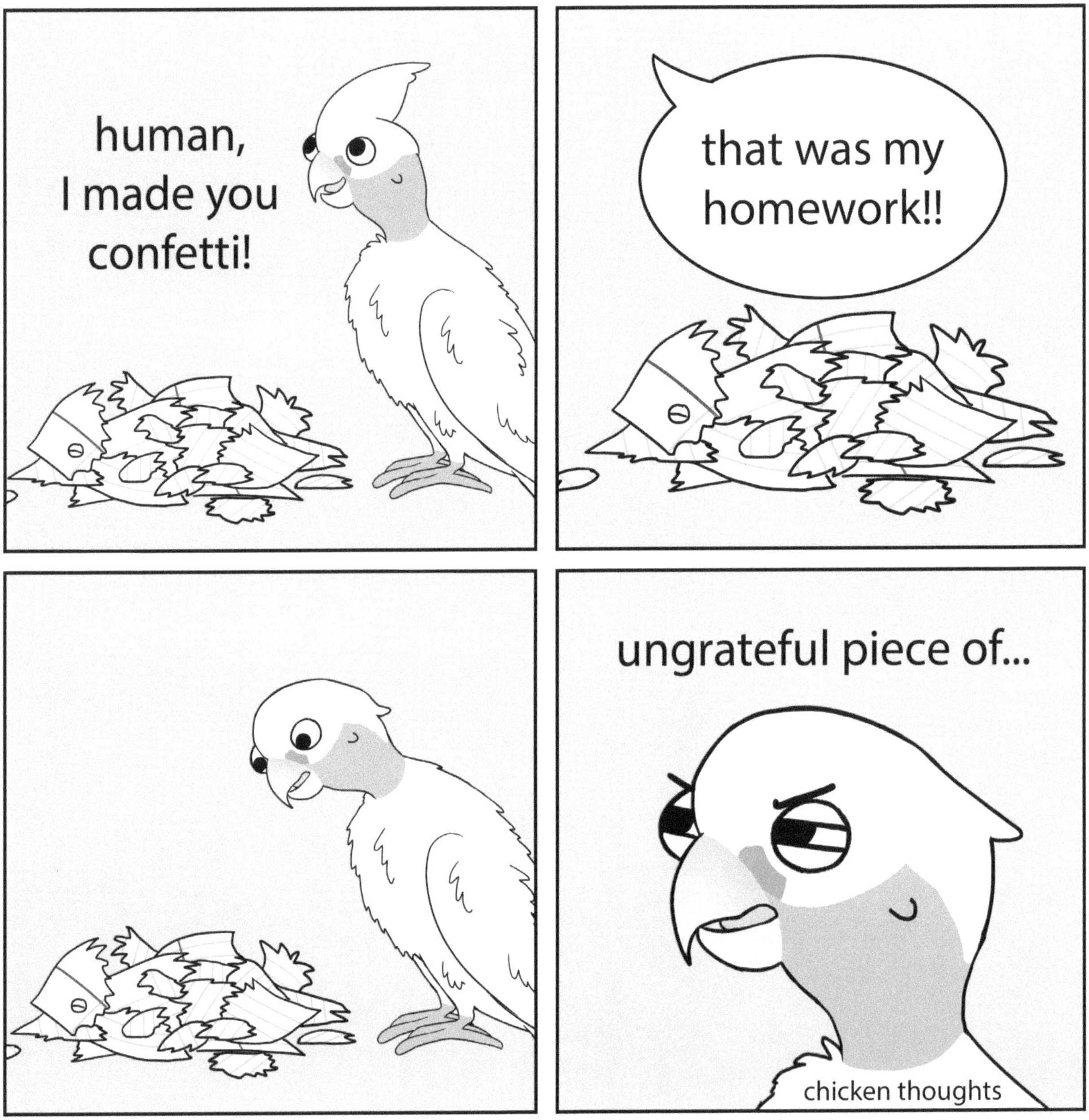
human,
I made you
confetti!
that was my
homework!!
ungrateful piece of...
chicken thoughts

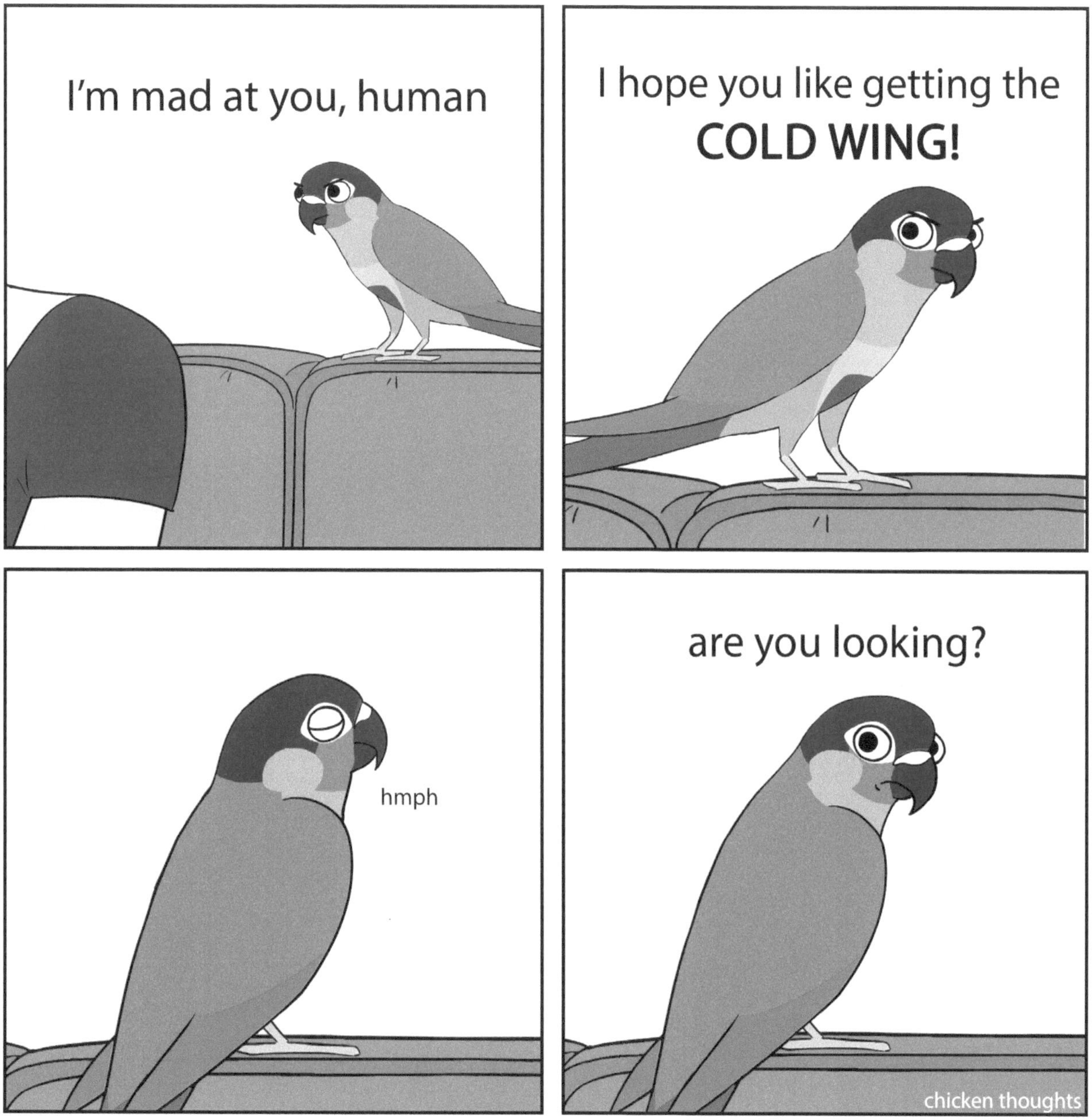
I'm mad at you, human
I hope you like getting the
COLD WING!
hmph
are you looking?
chicken thoughts

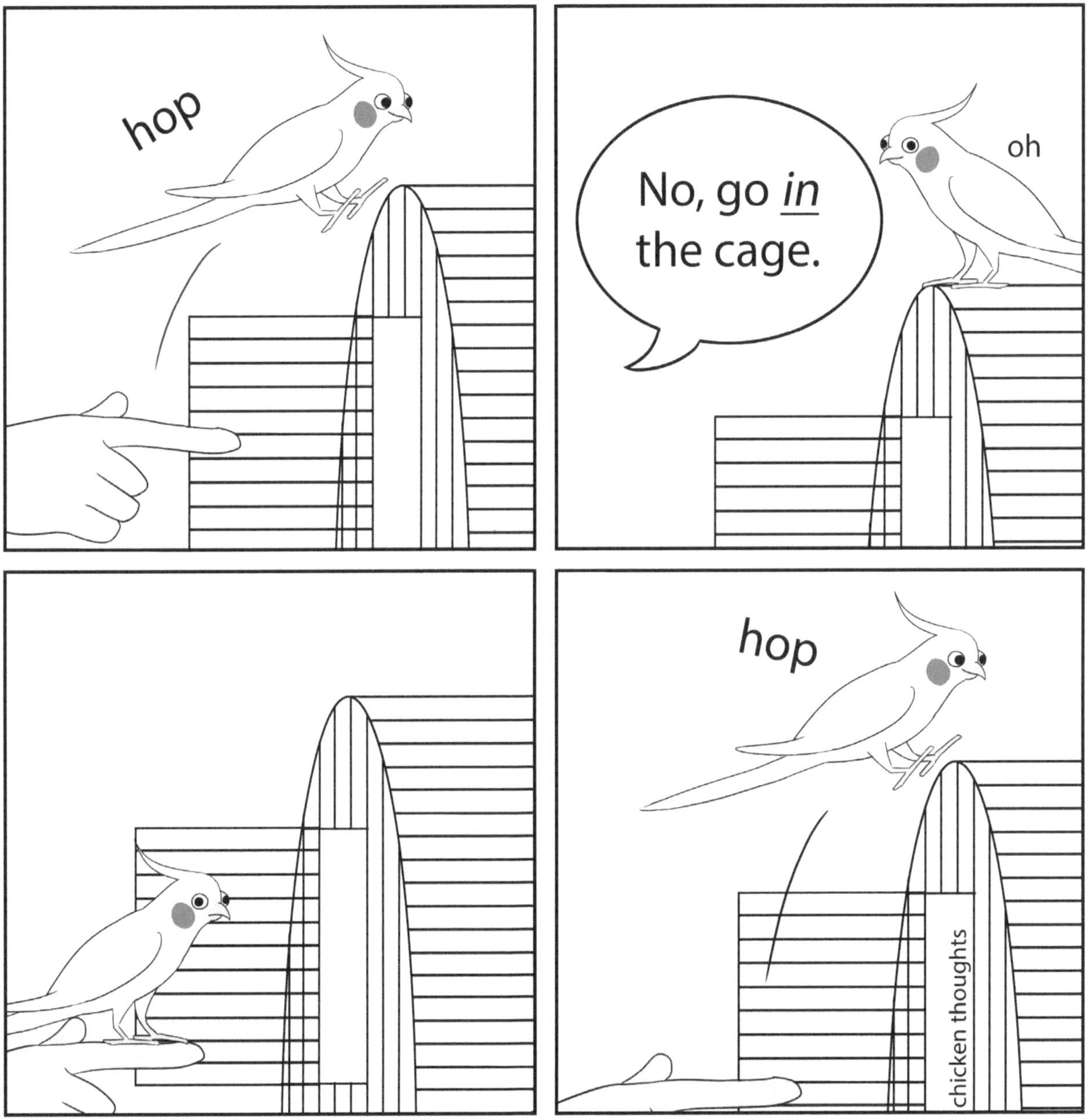
hop
No, go *in* the cage.
oh
hop
chicken thoughts

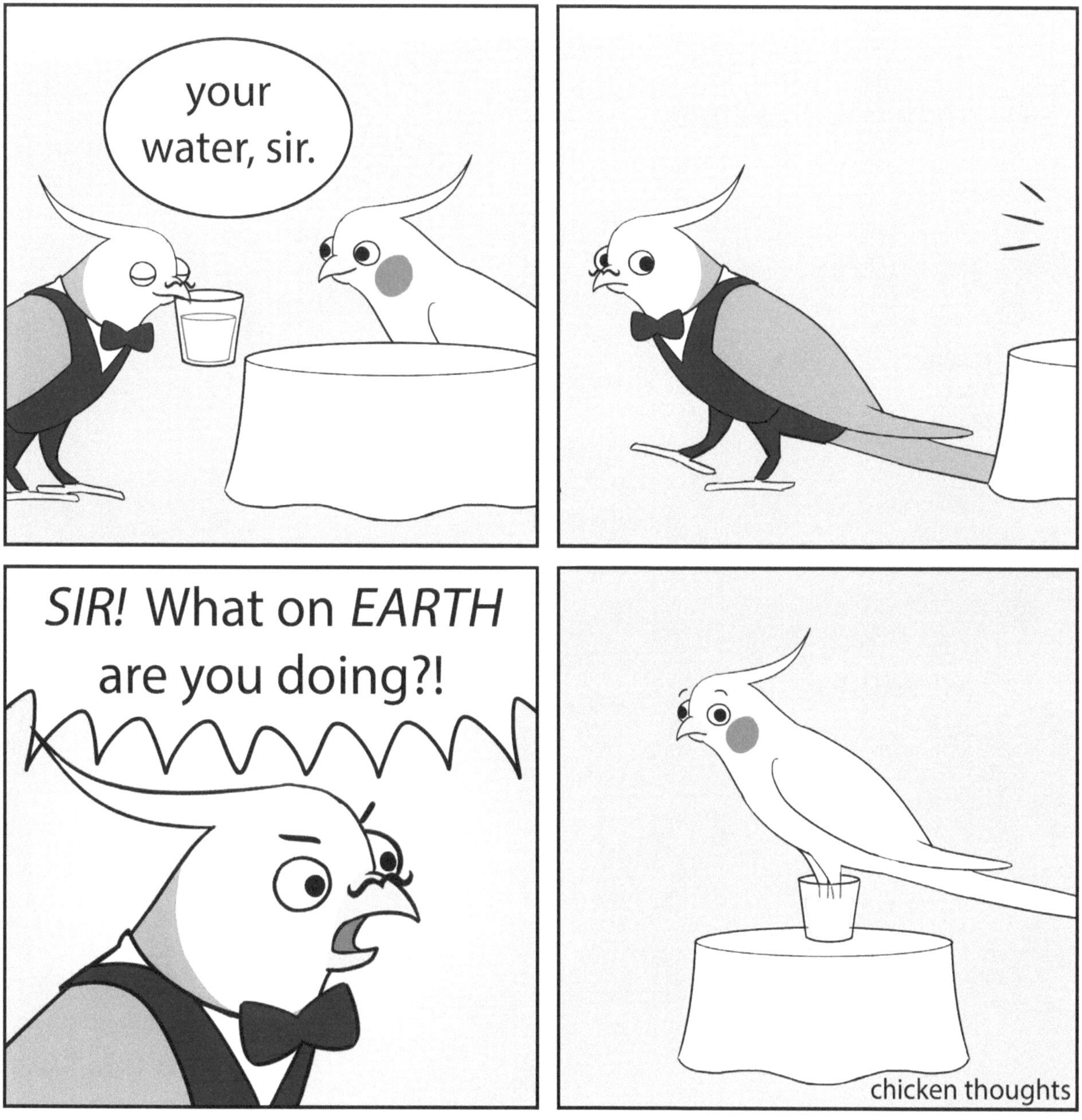
your water, sir.
SIR! What on *EARTH* are you doing?!
chicken thoughts

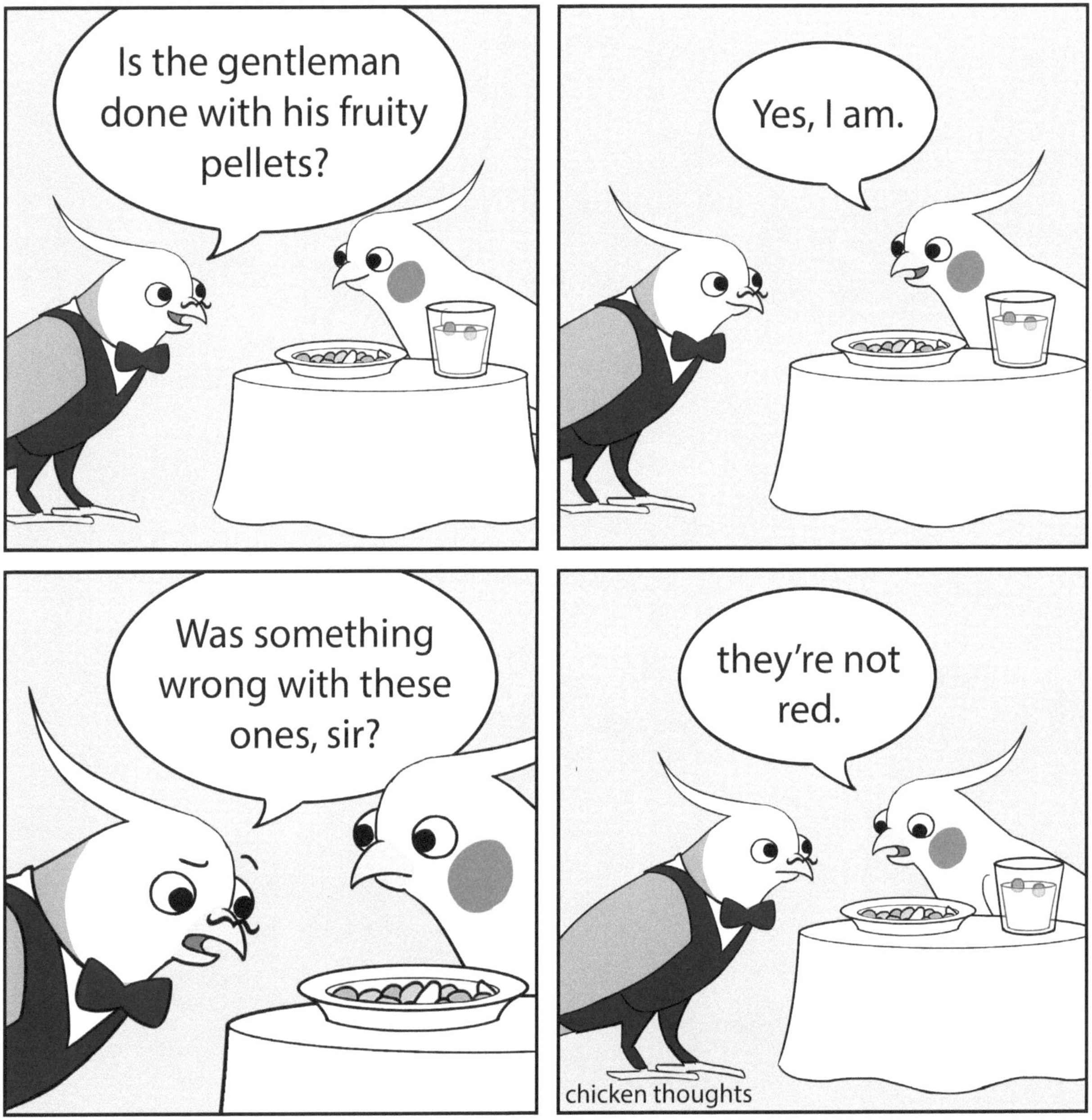
Is the gentleman done with his fruity pellets?
Yes, I am.
Was something wrong with these ones, sir?
they're not red.
chicken thoughts

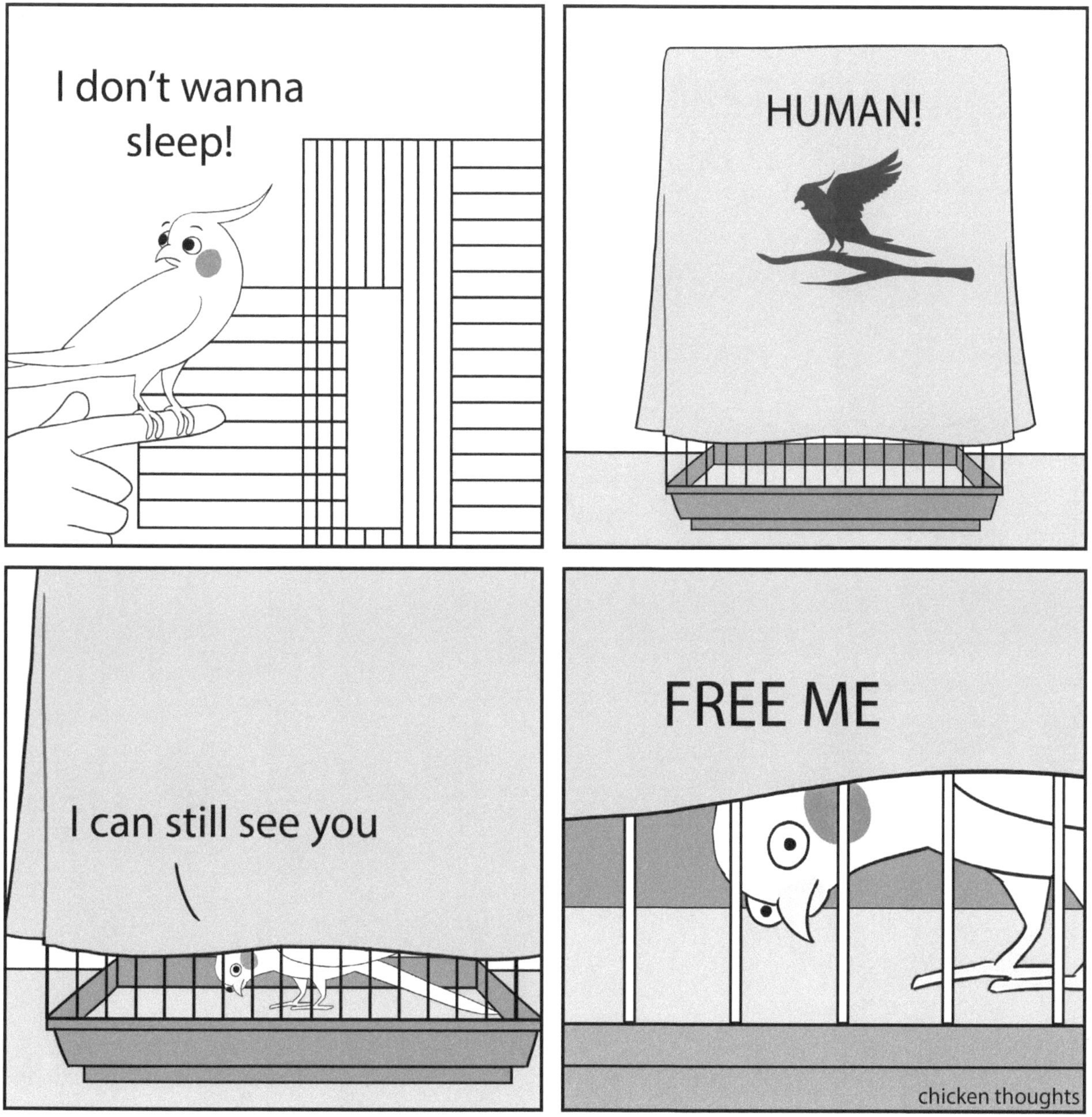
I don't wanna sleep!
HUMAN!
I can still see you
FREE ME
chicken thoughts

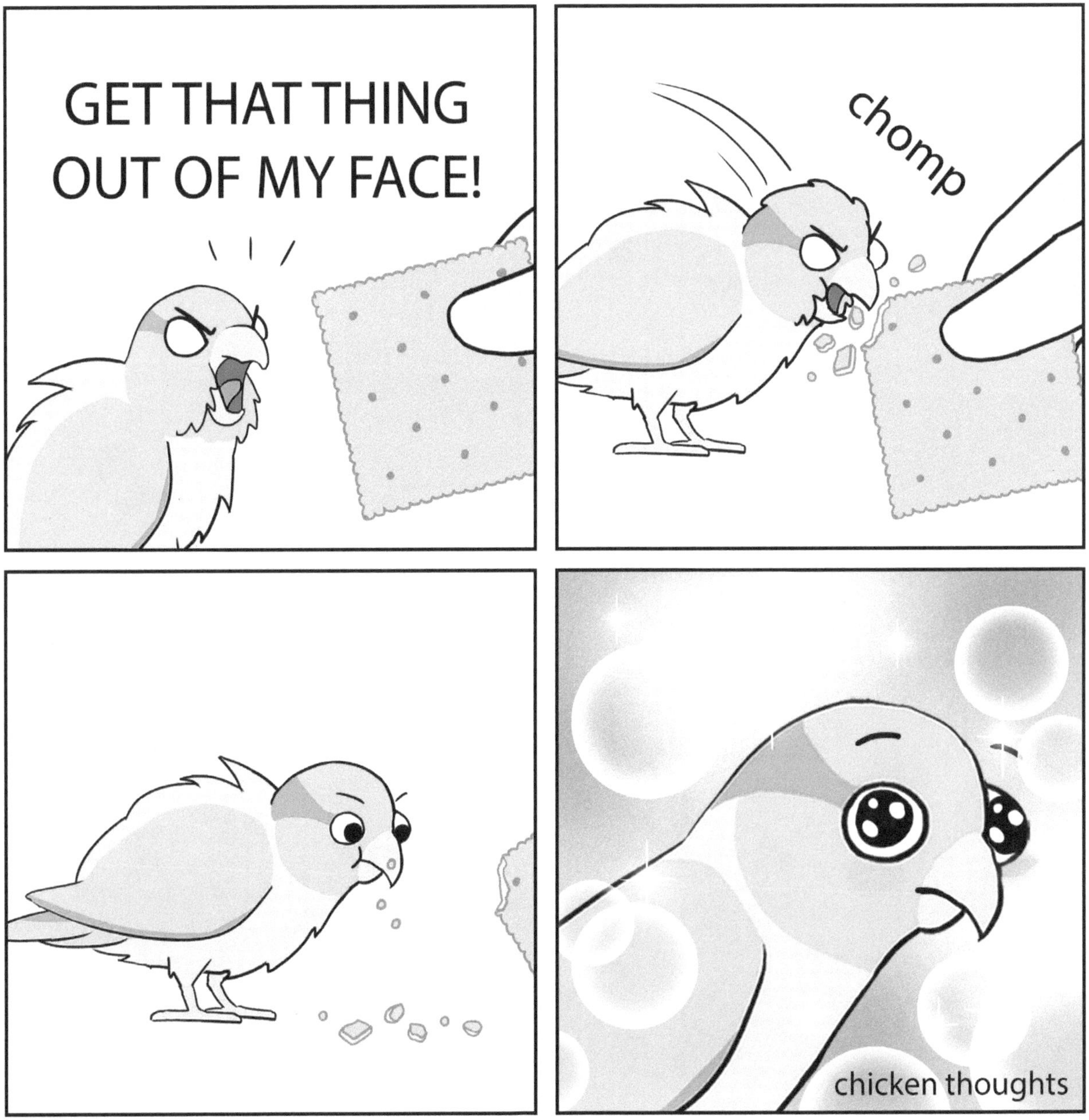
GET THAT THING
OUT OF MY FACE!
chomp
chicken thoughts

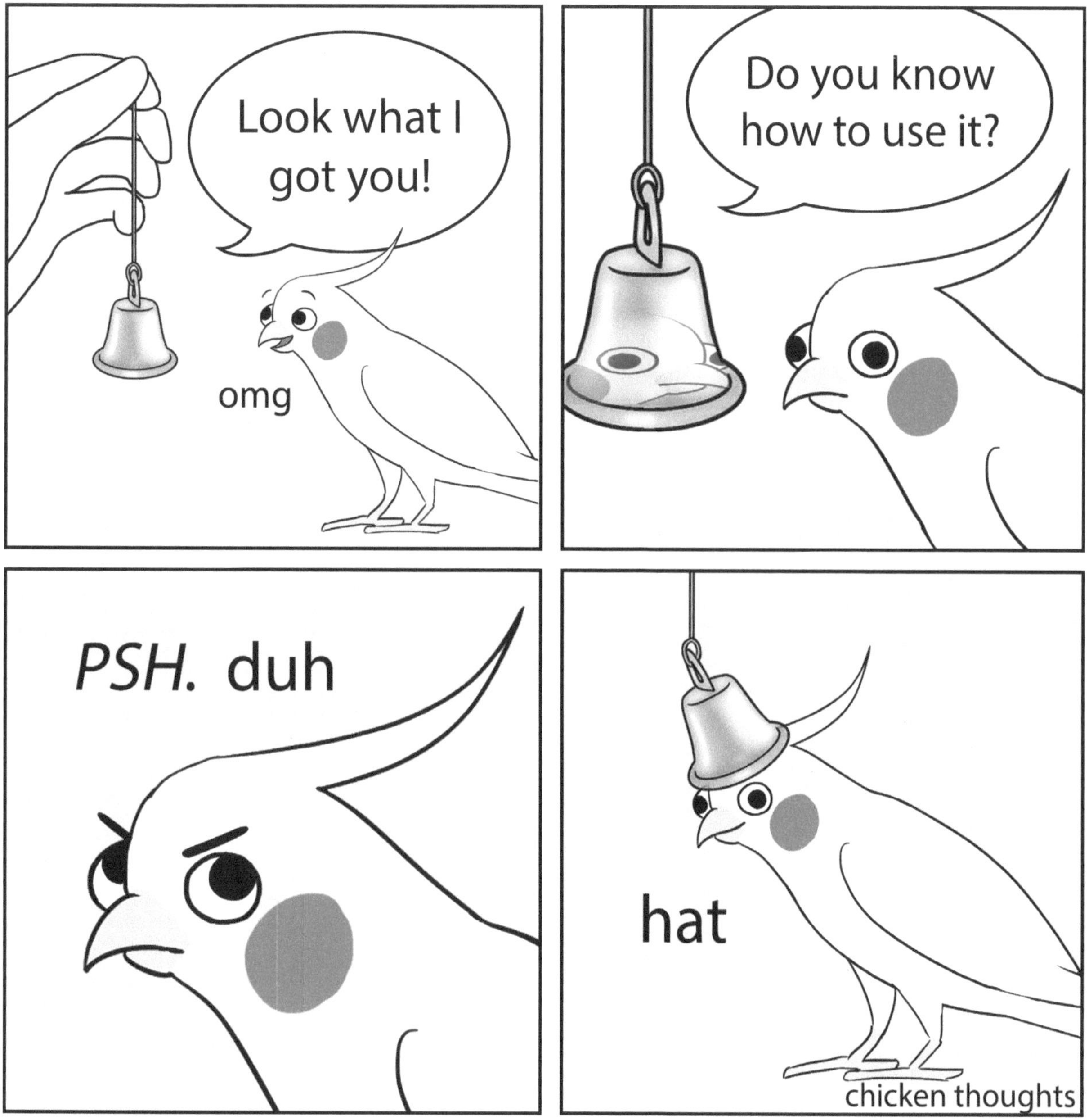
Look what I got you!
omg
Do you know how to use it?
PSH. duh
hat
chicken thoughts

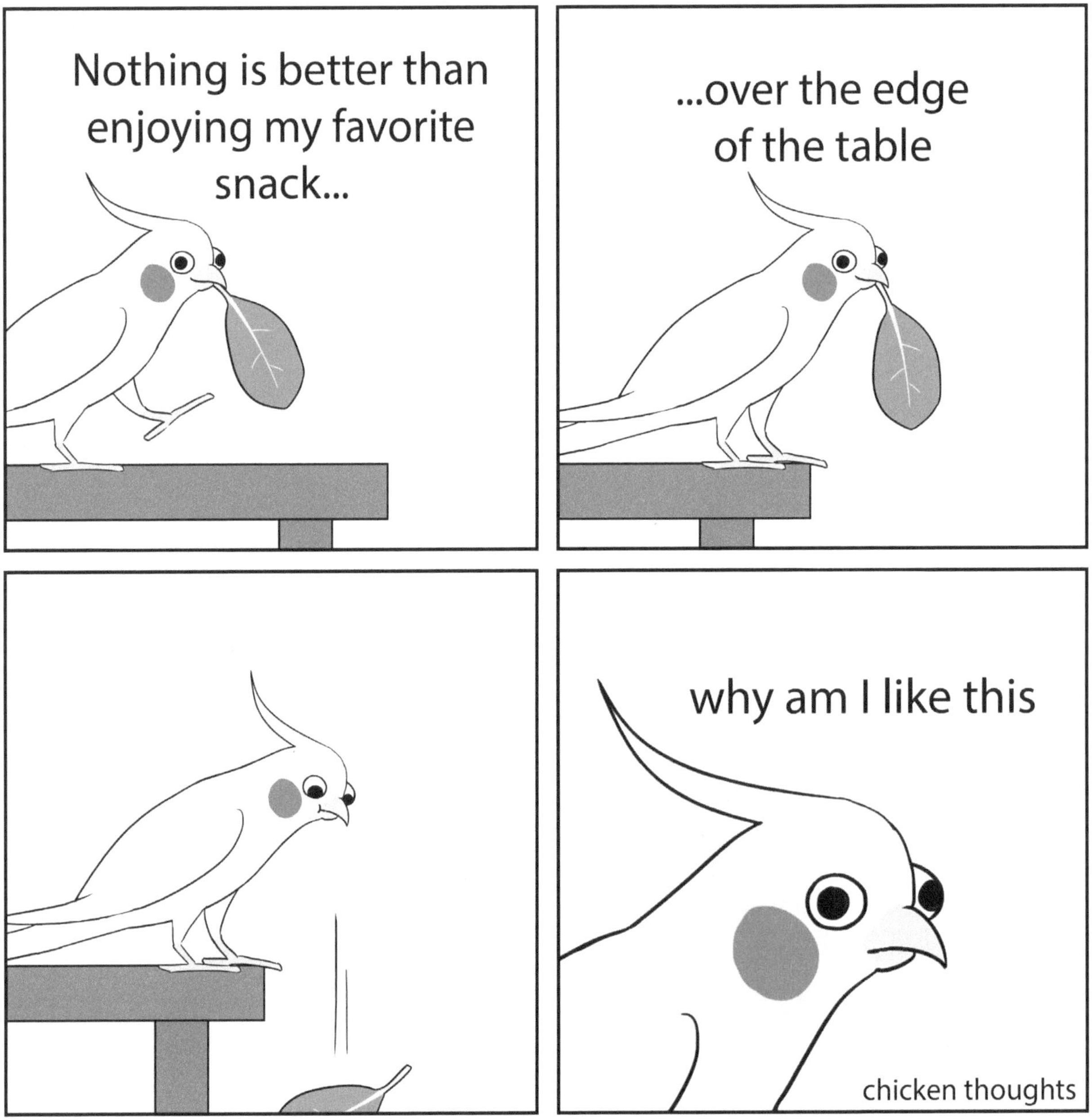
Nothing is better than enjoying my favorite snack...
...over the edge of the table
why am I like this
chicken thoughts

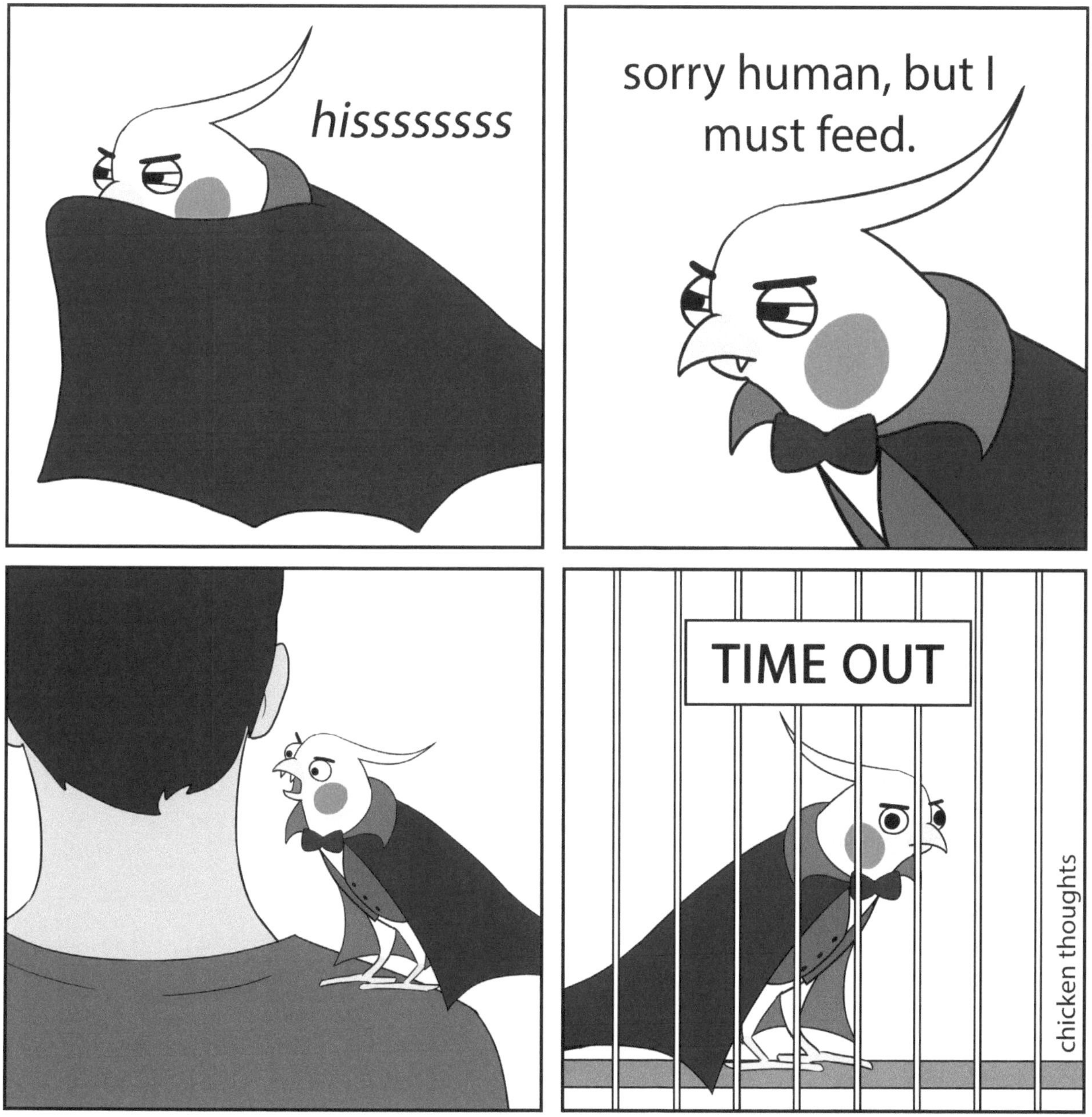
hisssssssss
sorry human, but I must feed.
TIME OUT
chicken thoughts

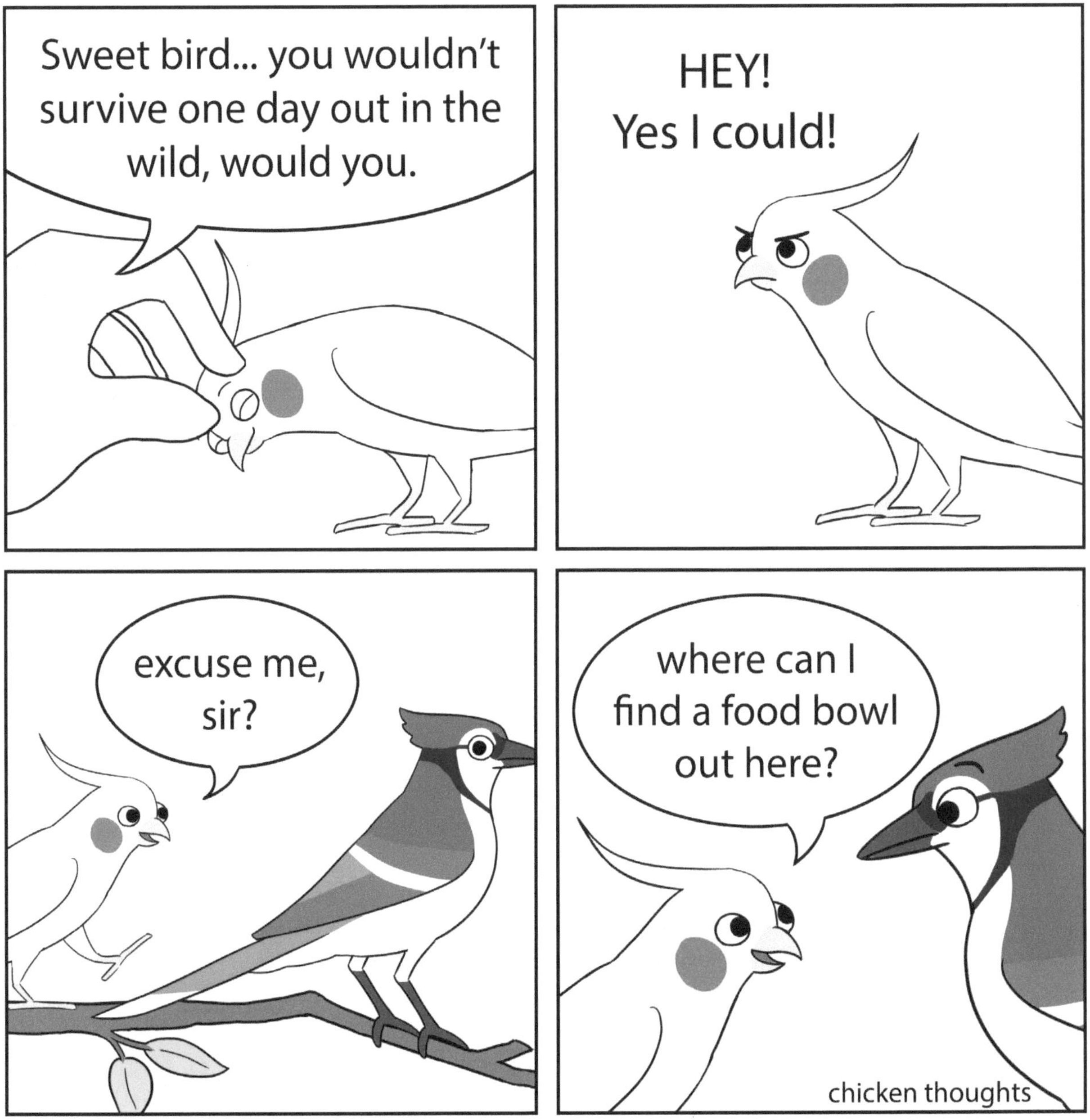
Sweet bird... you wouldn't survive one day out in the wild, would you.
HEY! Yes I could!
excuse me, sir?
where can I find a food bowl out here?
chicken thoughts

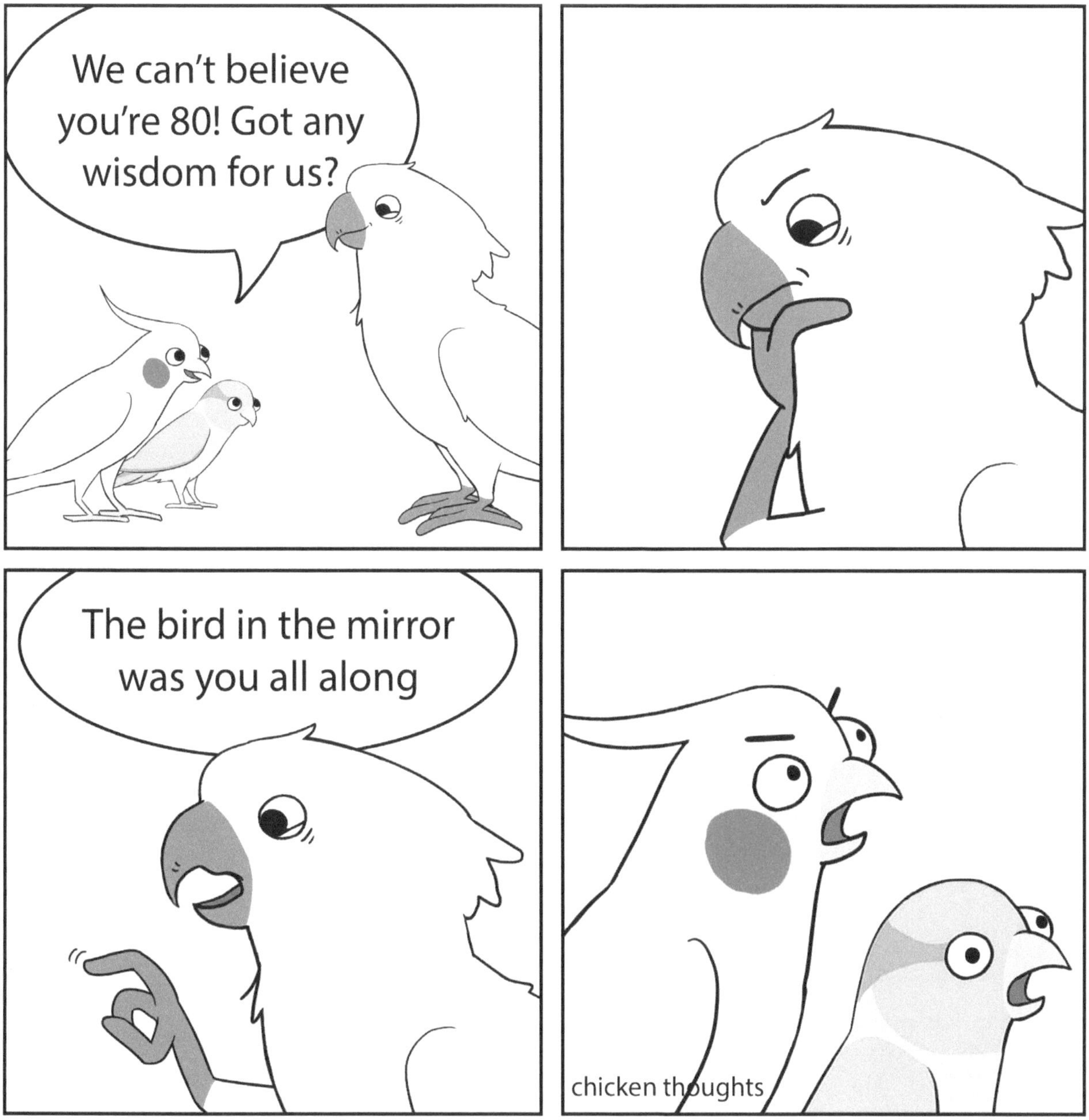
We can't believe you're 80! Got any wisdom for us?
The bird in the mirror was you all along
chicken thoughts

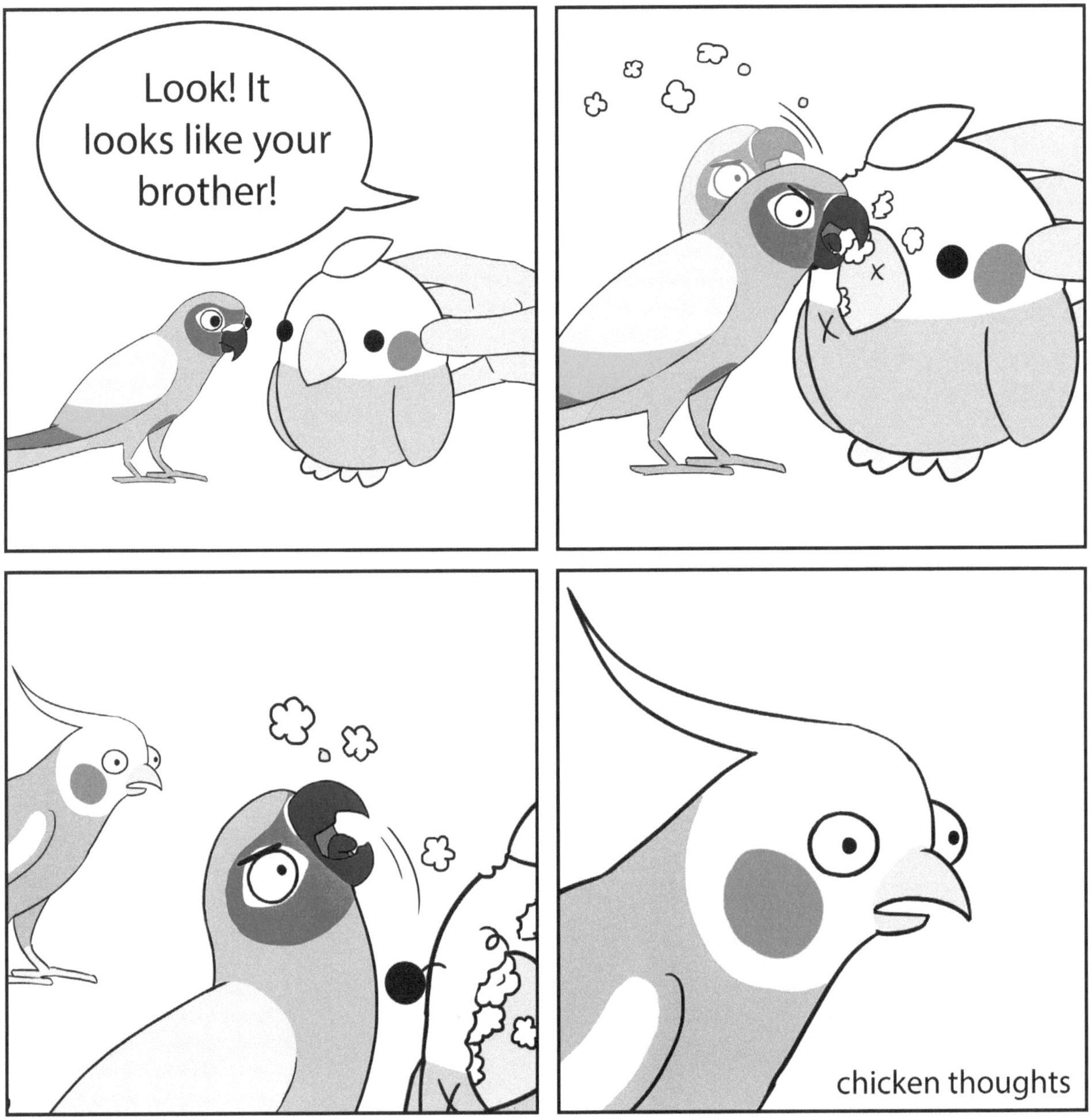
Look! It looks like your brother!
chicken thoughts

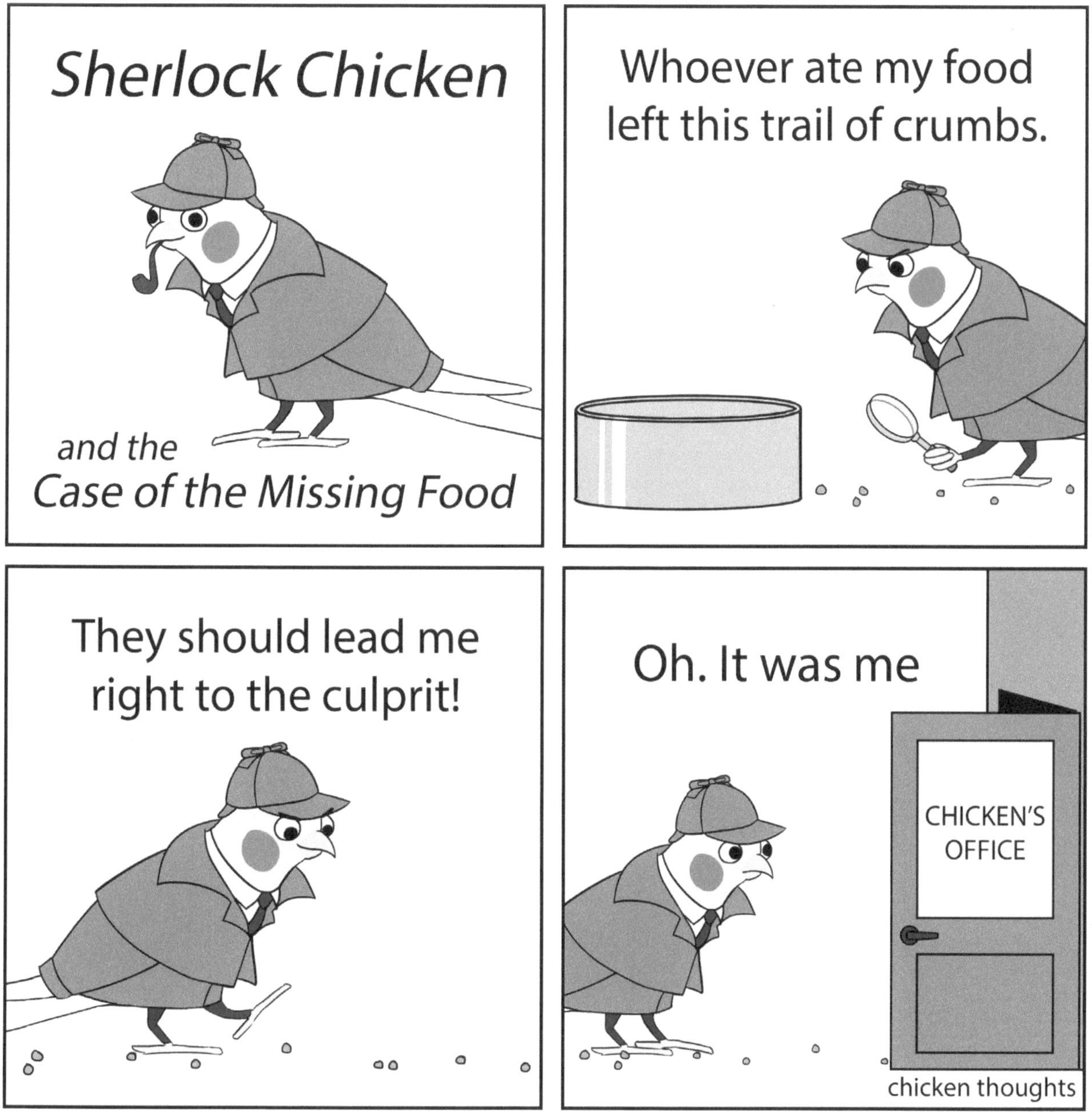
Sherlock Chicken
and the
Case of the Missing Food
Whoever ate my food left this trail of crumbs.
They should lead me right to the culprit!
Oh. It was me
CHICKEN'S OFFICE
chicken thoughts

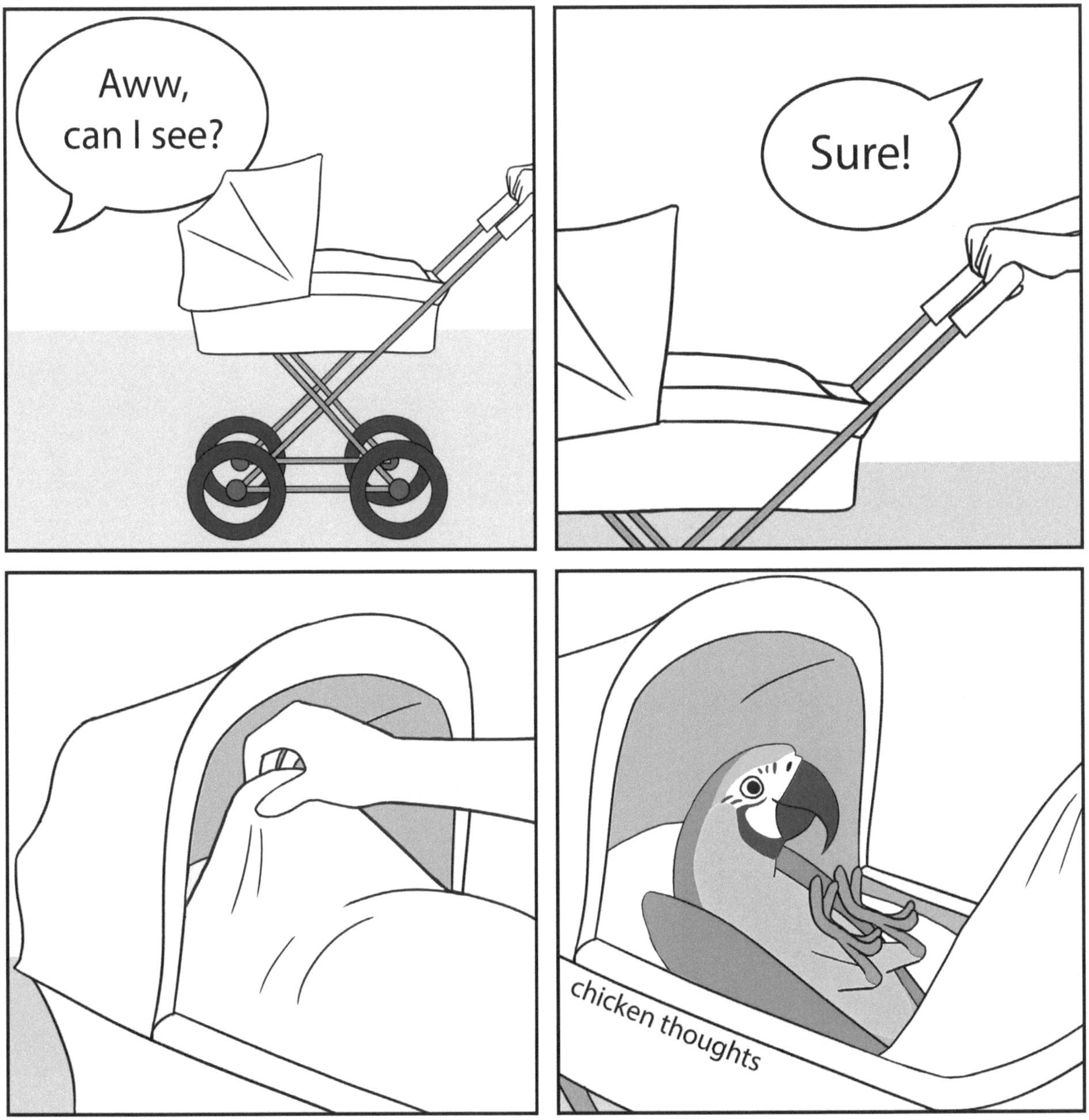
Aww,
can I see?
Sure!
chicken thoughts

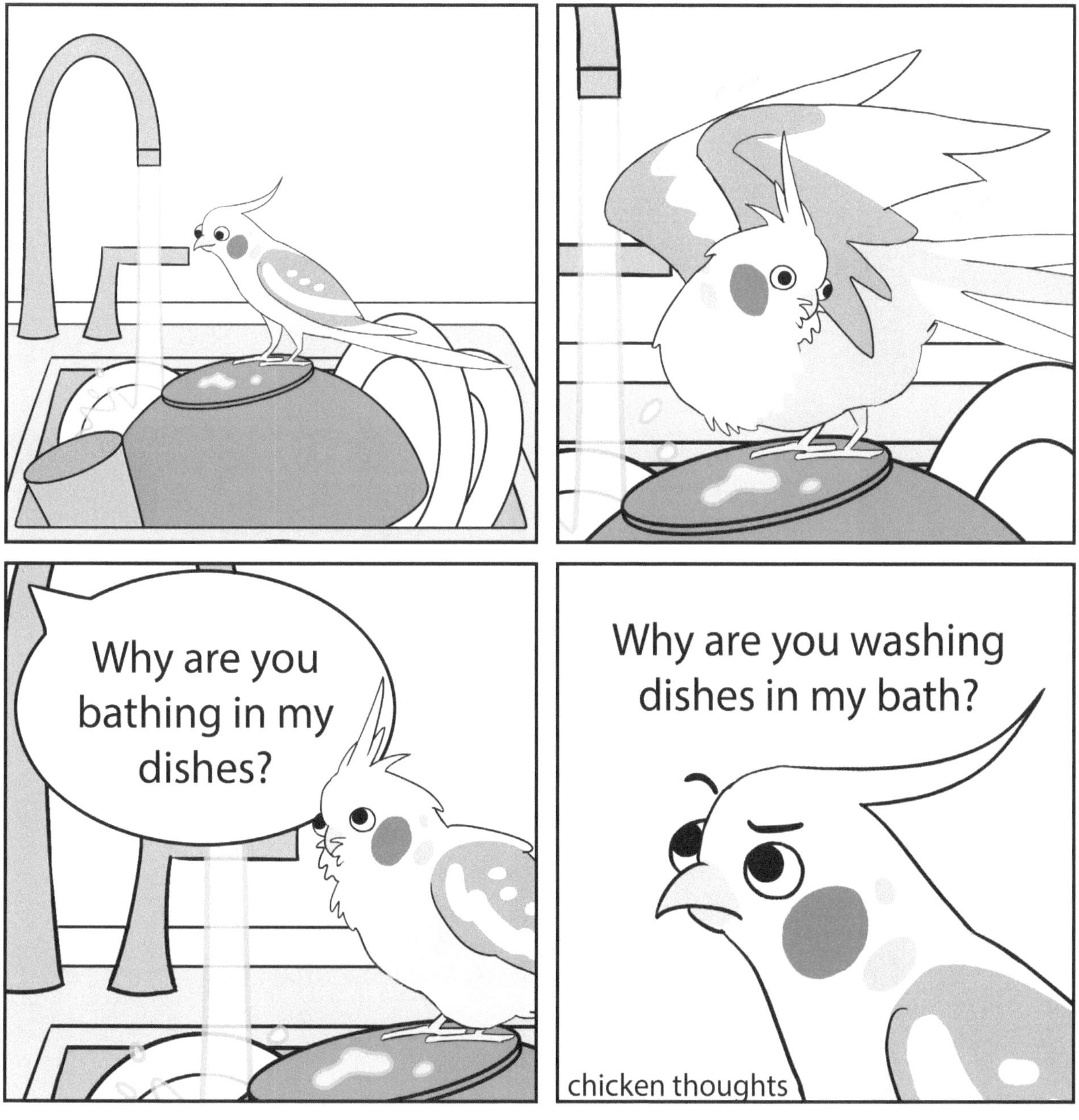
Why are you bathing in my dishes?
Why are you washing dishes in my bath?
chicken thoughts

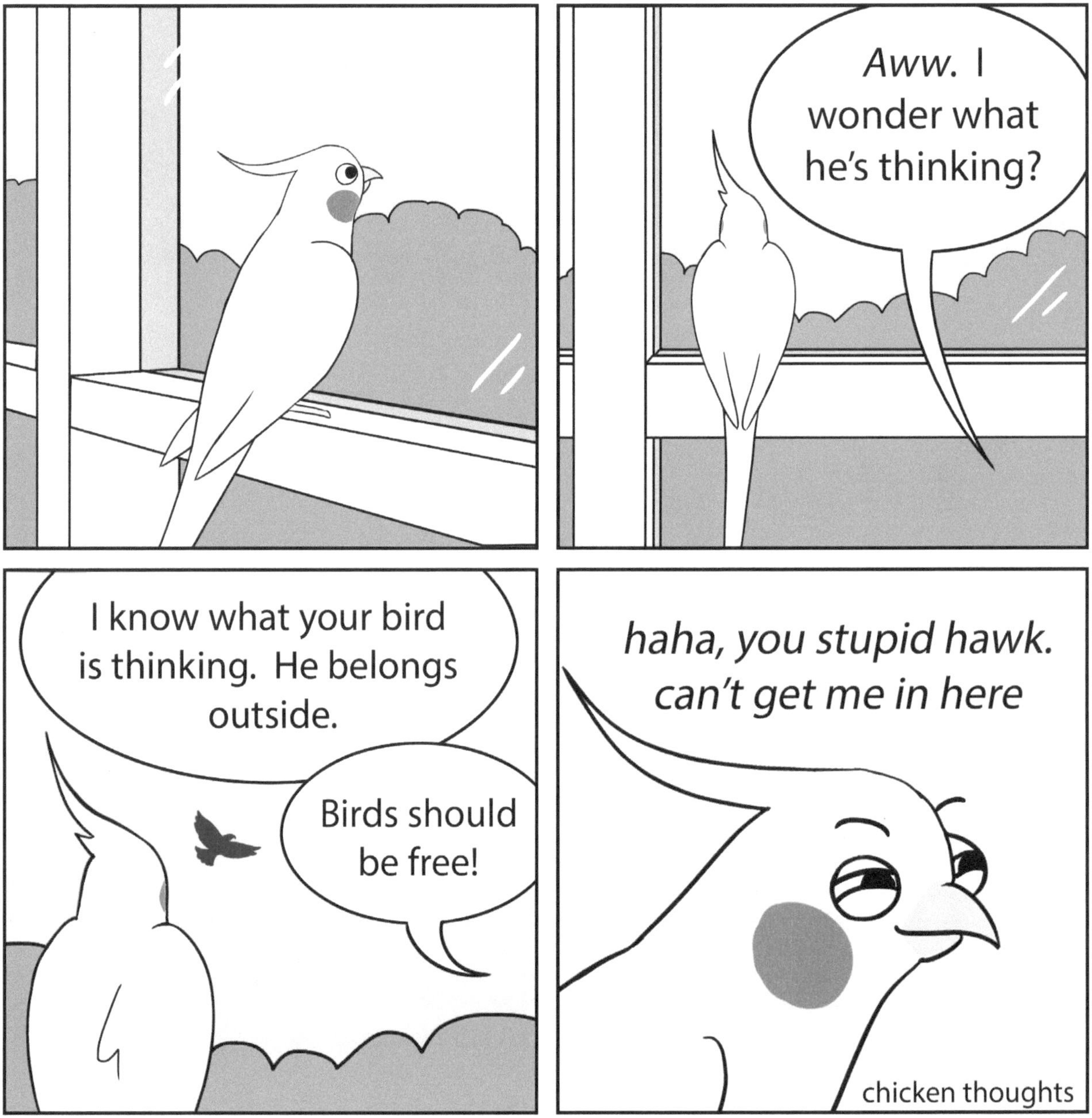
Aww. I wonder what he's thinking?
I know what your bird is thinking. He belongs outside.
Birds should be free!
haha, you stupid hawk. can't get me in here
chicken thoughts

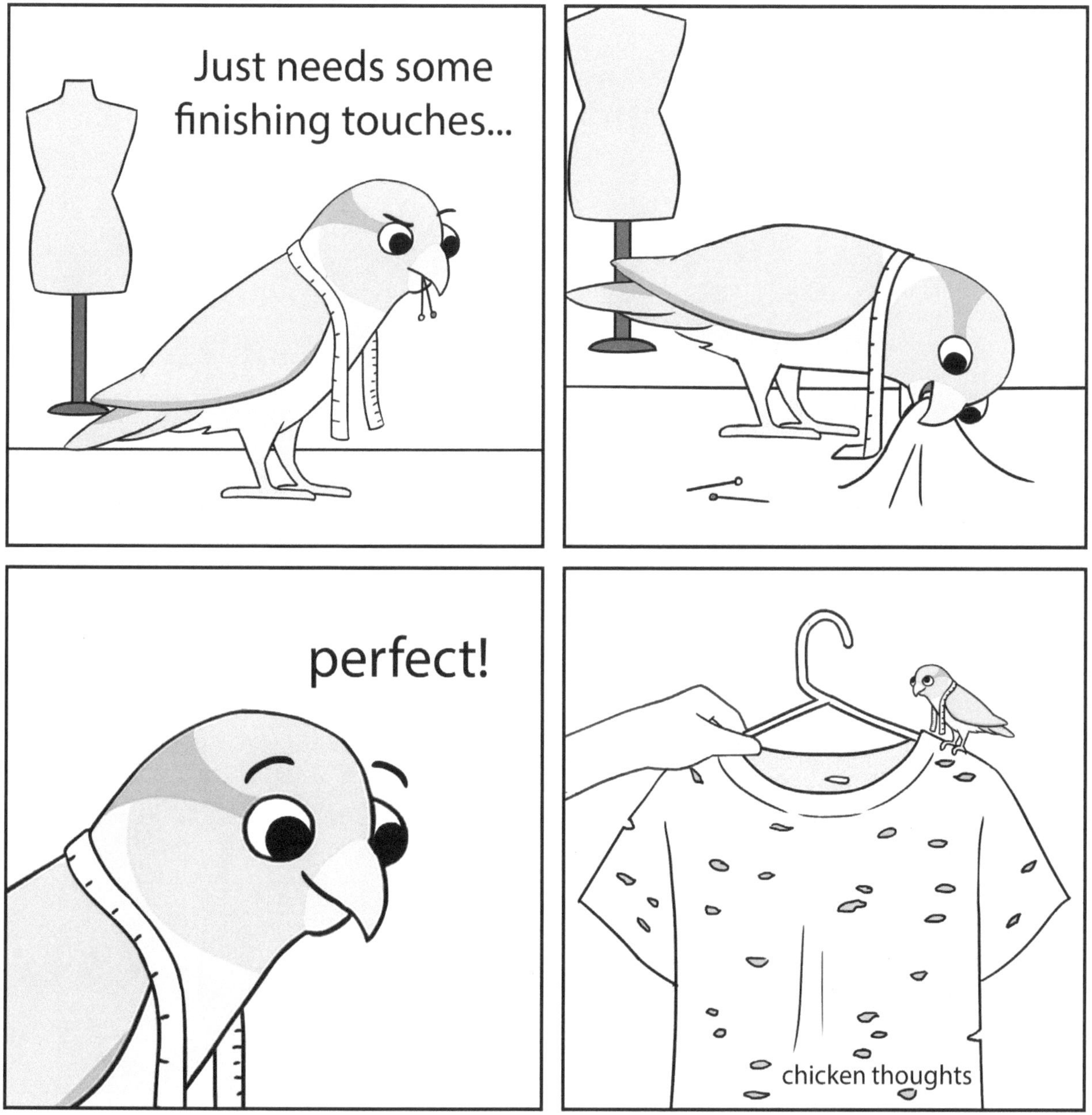
Just needs some finishing touches...
perfect!
chicken thoughts

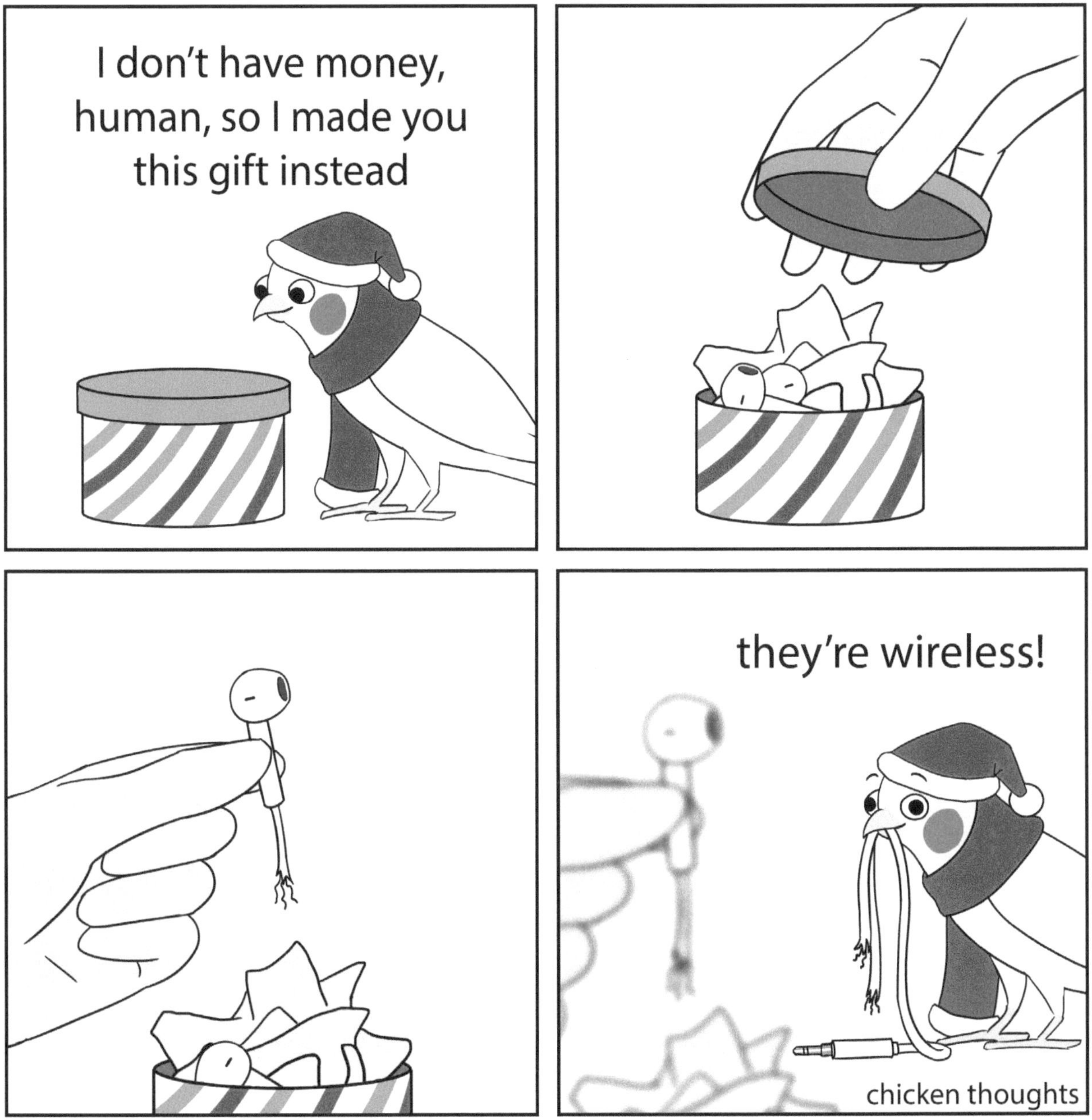
I don't have money, human, so I made you this gift instead
they're wireless!
chicken thoughts

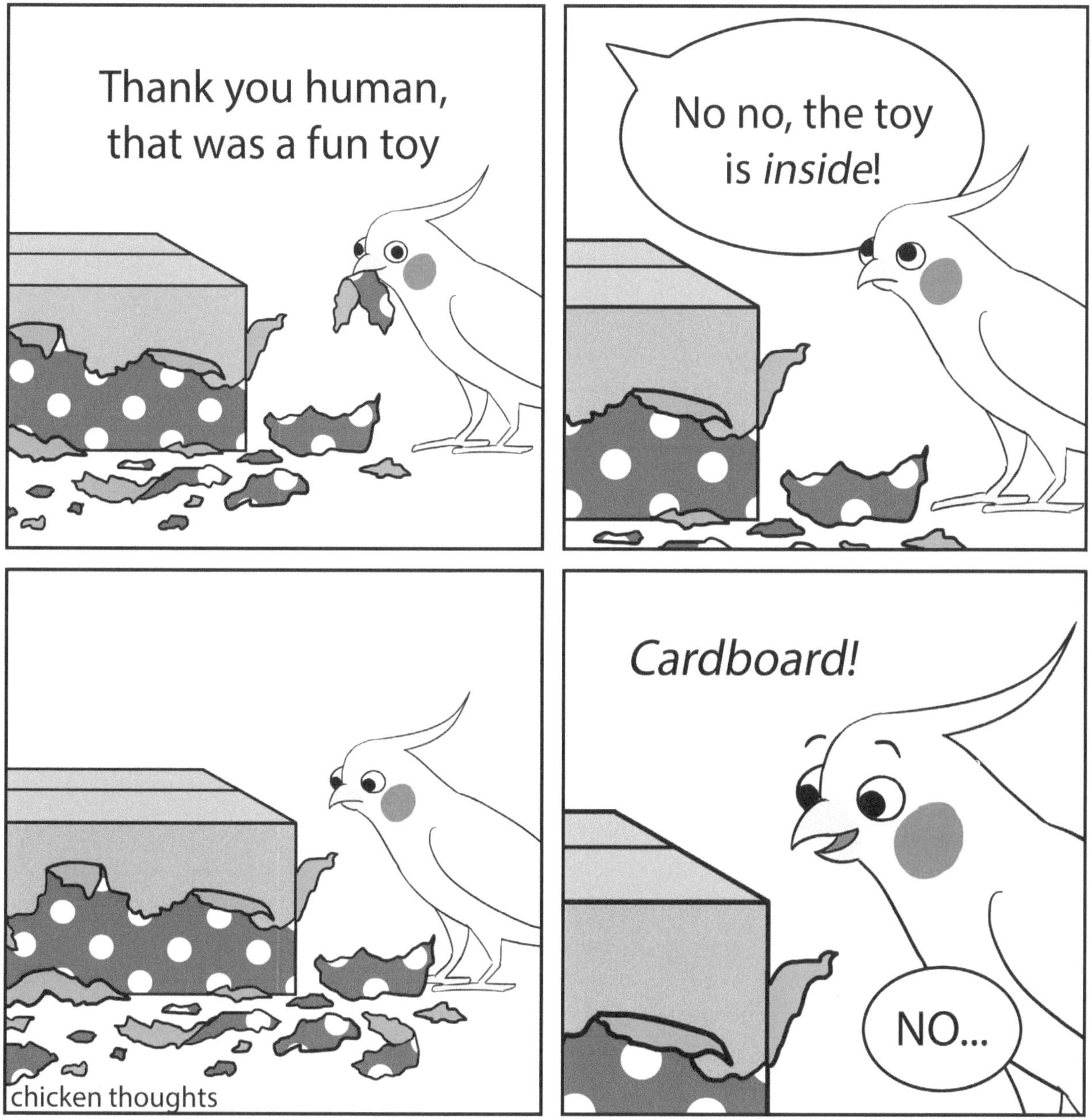
Thank you human, that was a fun toy
No no, the toy is *inside*!
Cardboard!
NO...
chicken thoughts

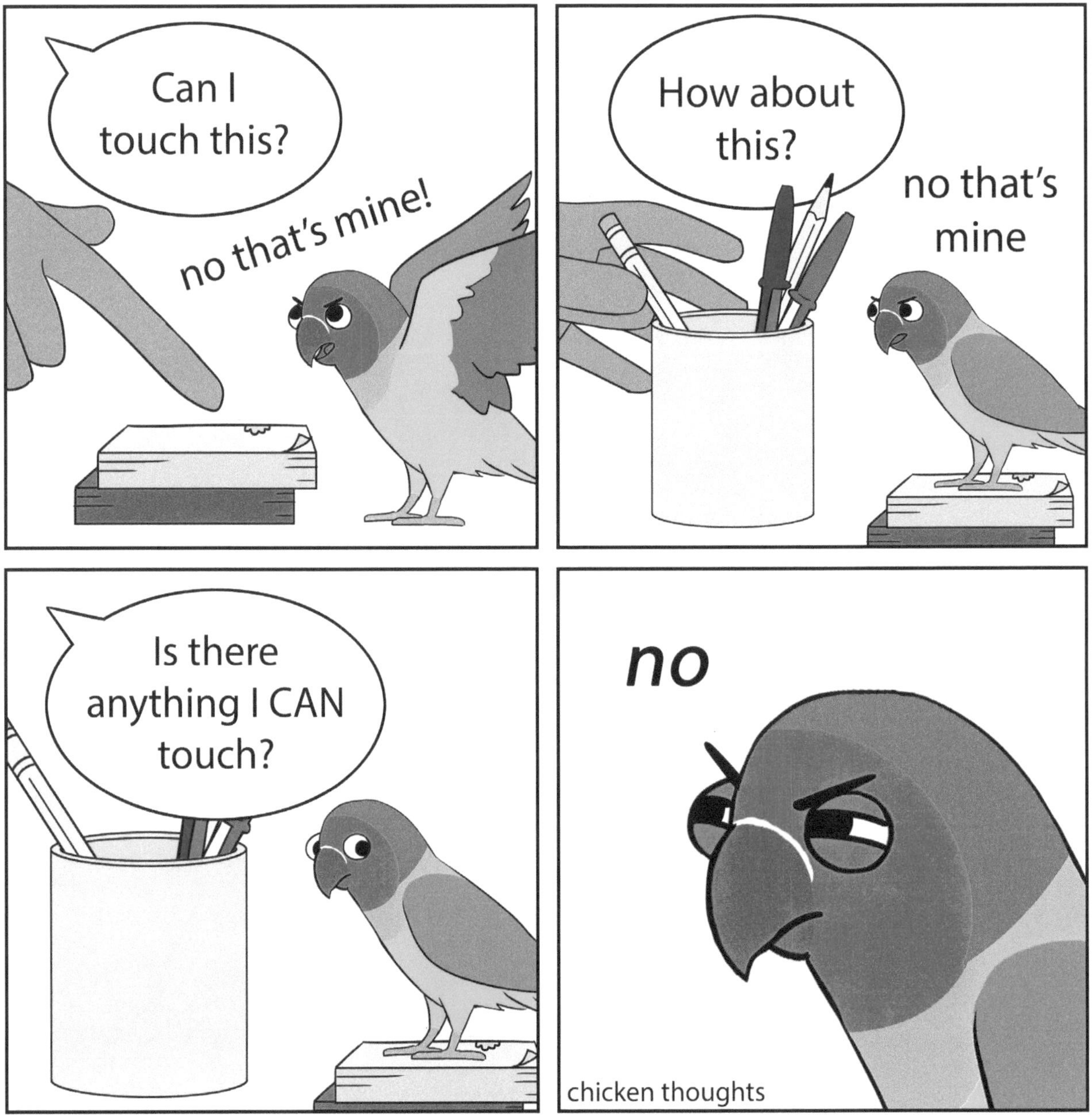
Can I touch this?
no that's mine!
How about this?
no that's mine
Is there anything I CAN touch?
no
chicken thoughts

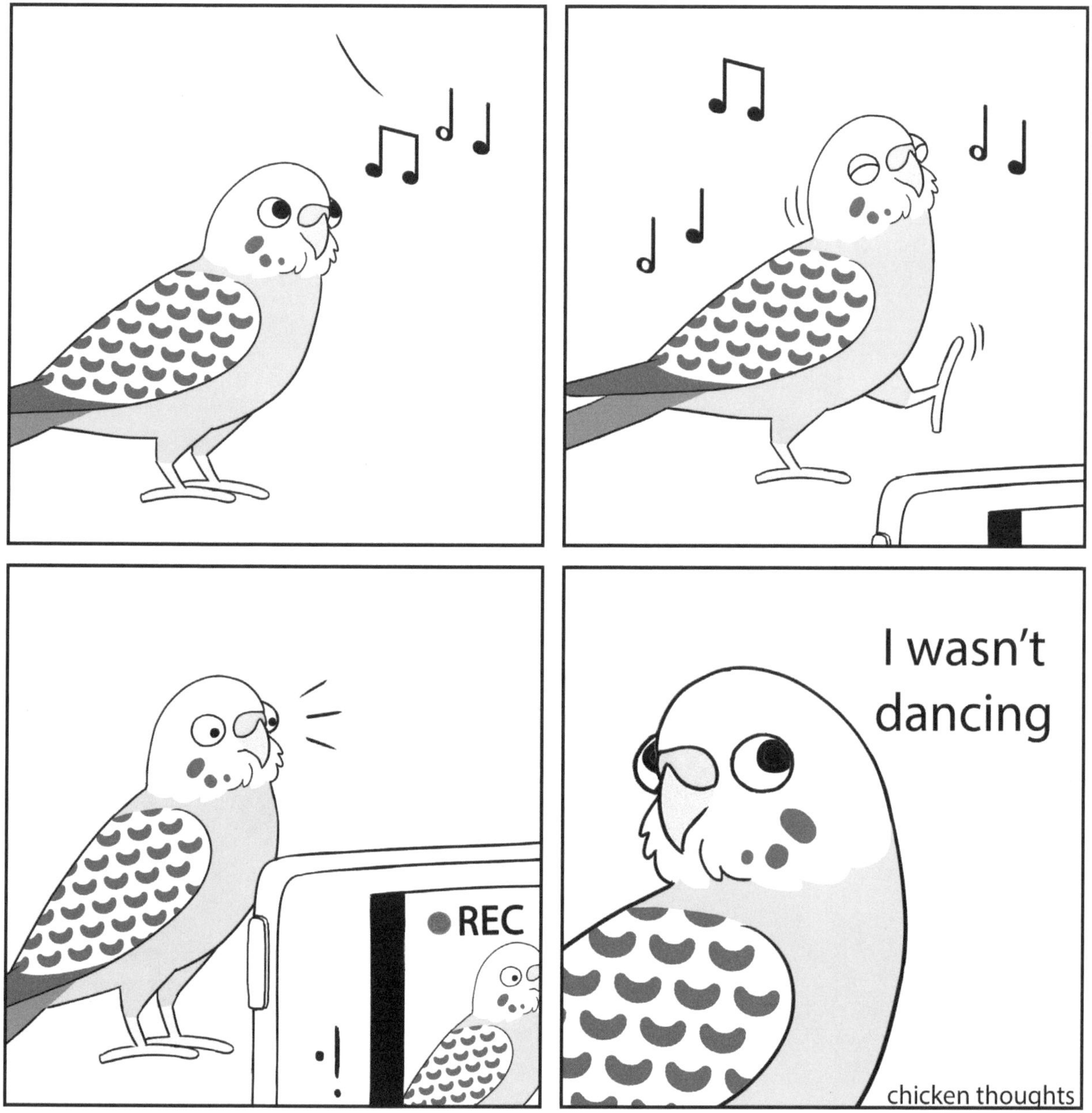
REC
I wasn't dancing
chicken thoughts

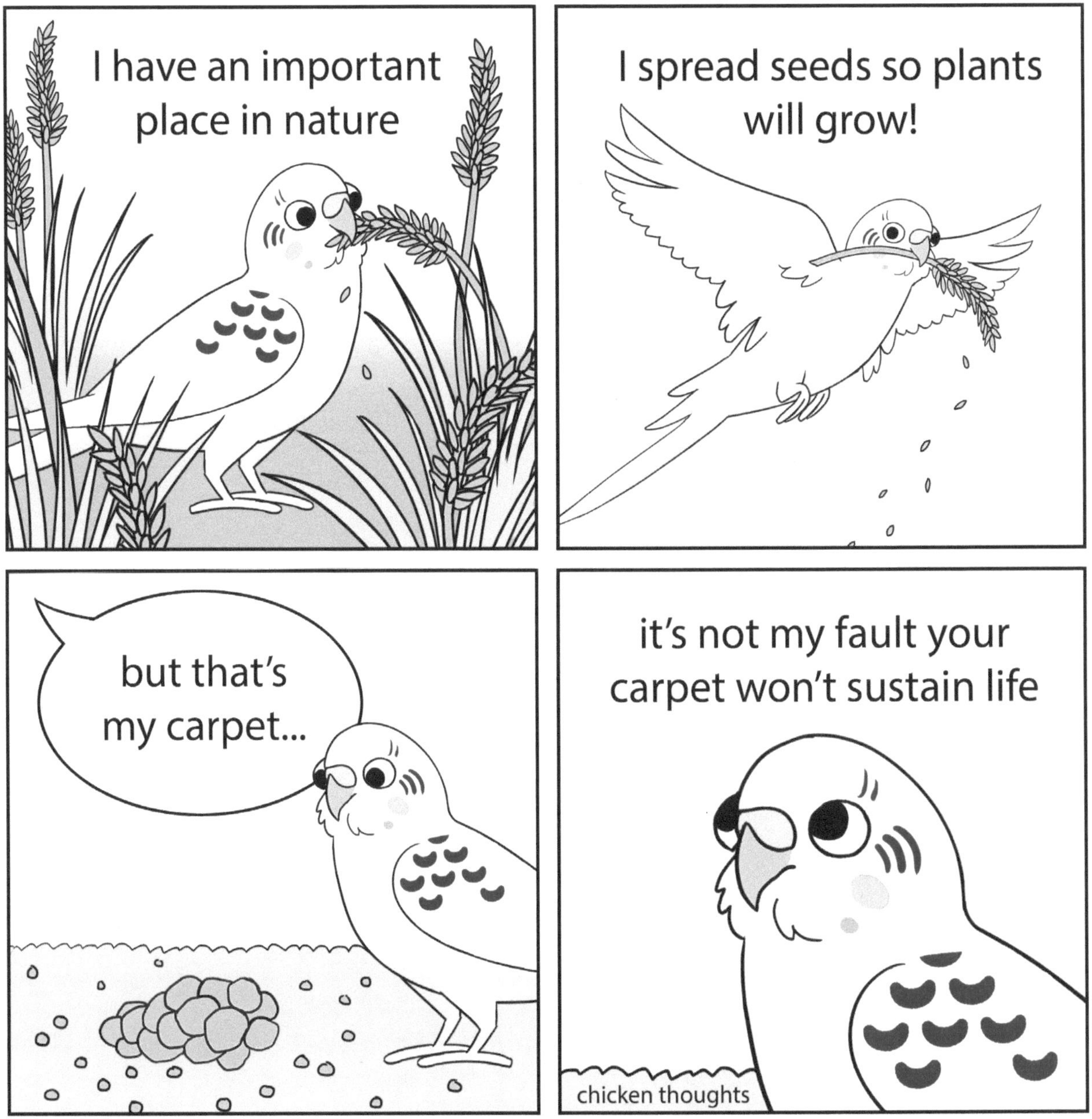
I have an important place in nature
I spread seeds so plants will grow!
but that's my carpet...
it's not my fault your carpet won't sustain life
chicken thoughts

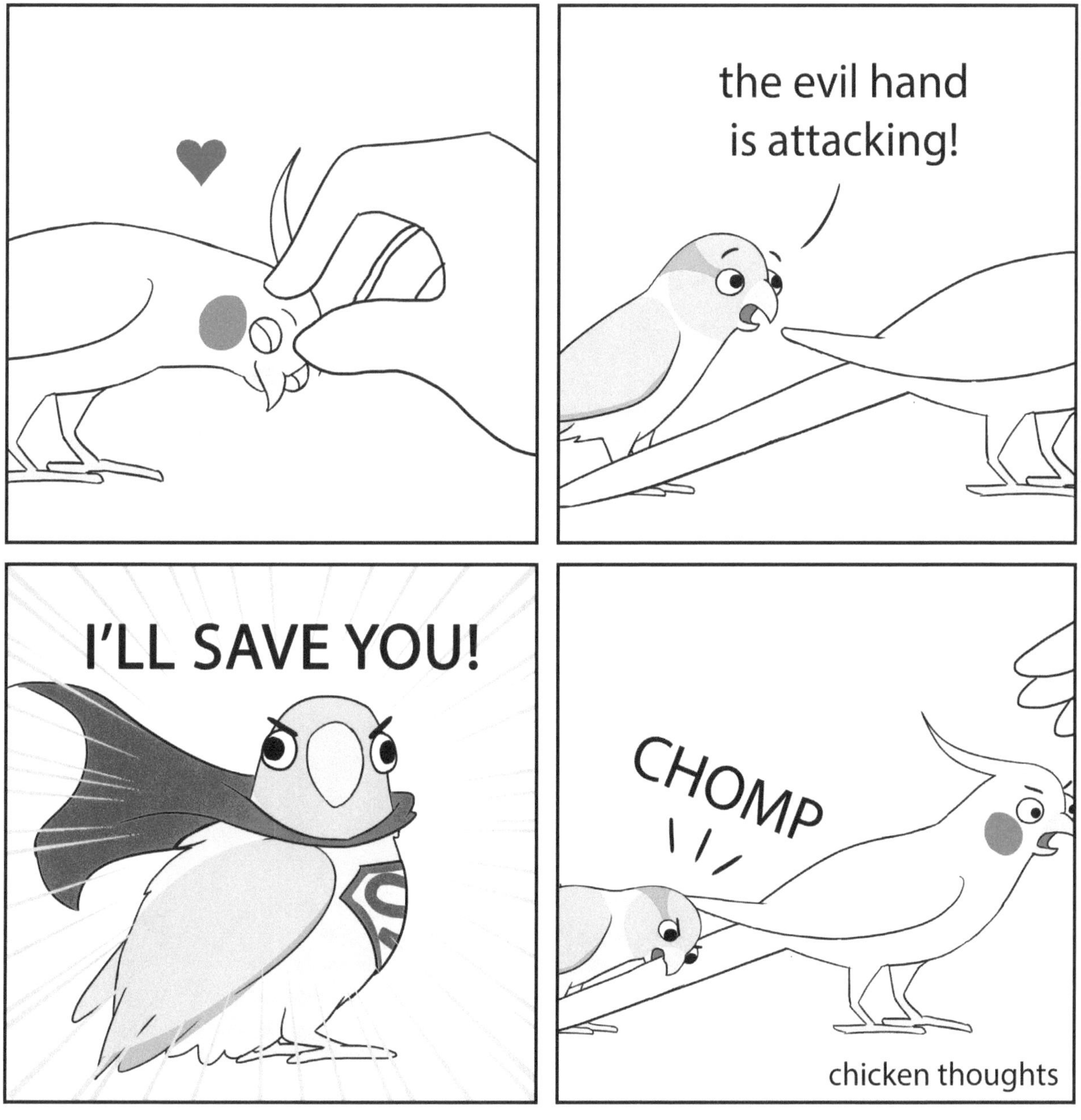
the evil hand
is attacking!
I'LL SAVE YOU!
CHOMP
chicken thoughts

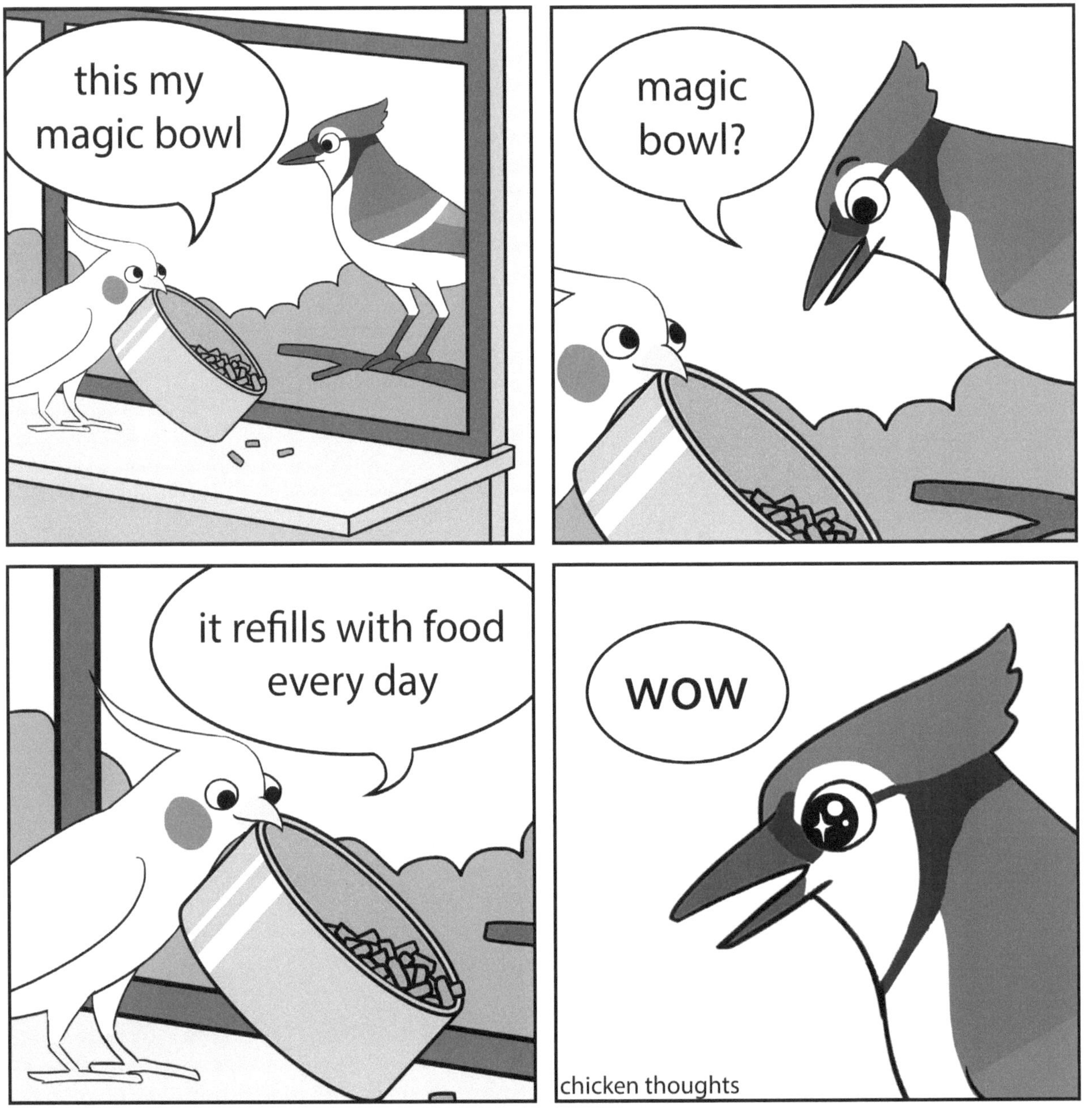
this my magic bowl
magic bowl?
it refills with food every day
wow
chicken thoughts

It's too quiet. Where is the bird?
POTATO CHEEPS
POTATO CHEEPS
chicken thoughts

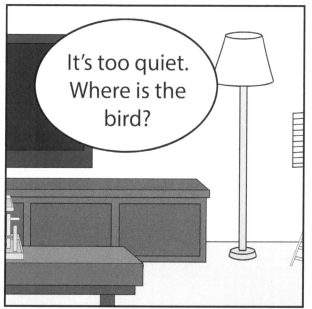

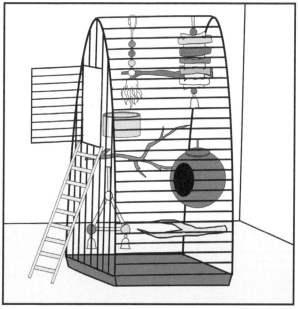

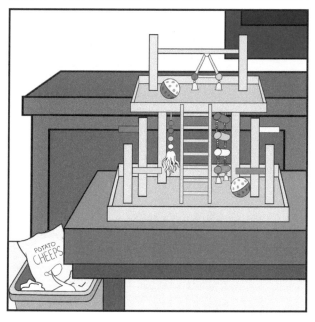

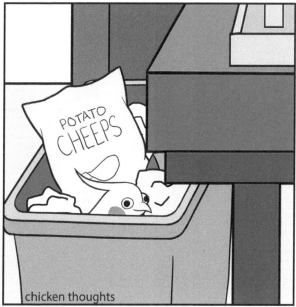

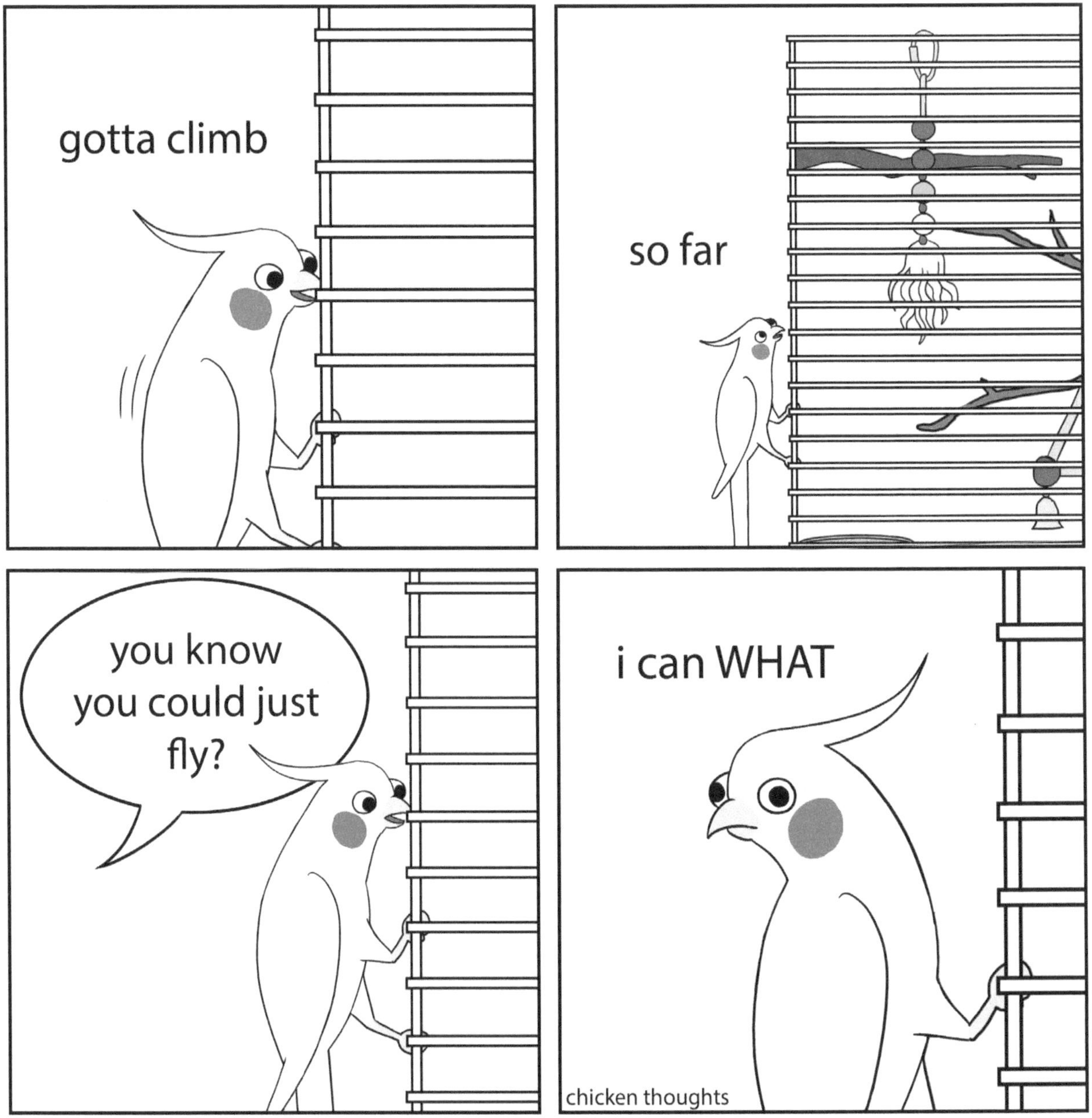
gotta climb
so far
you know you could just fly?
i can WHAT
chicken thoughts

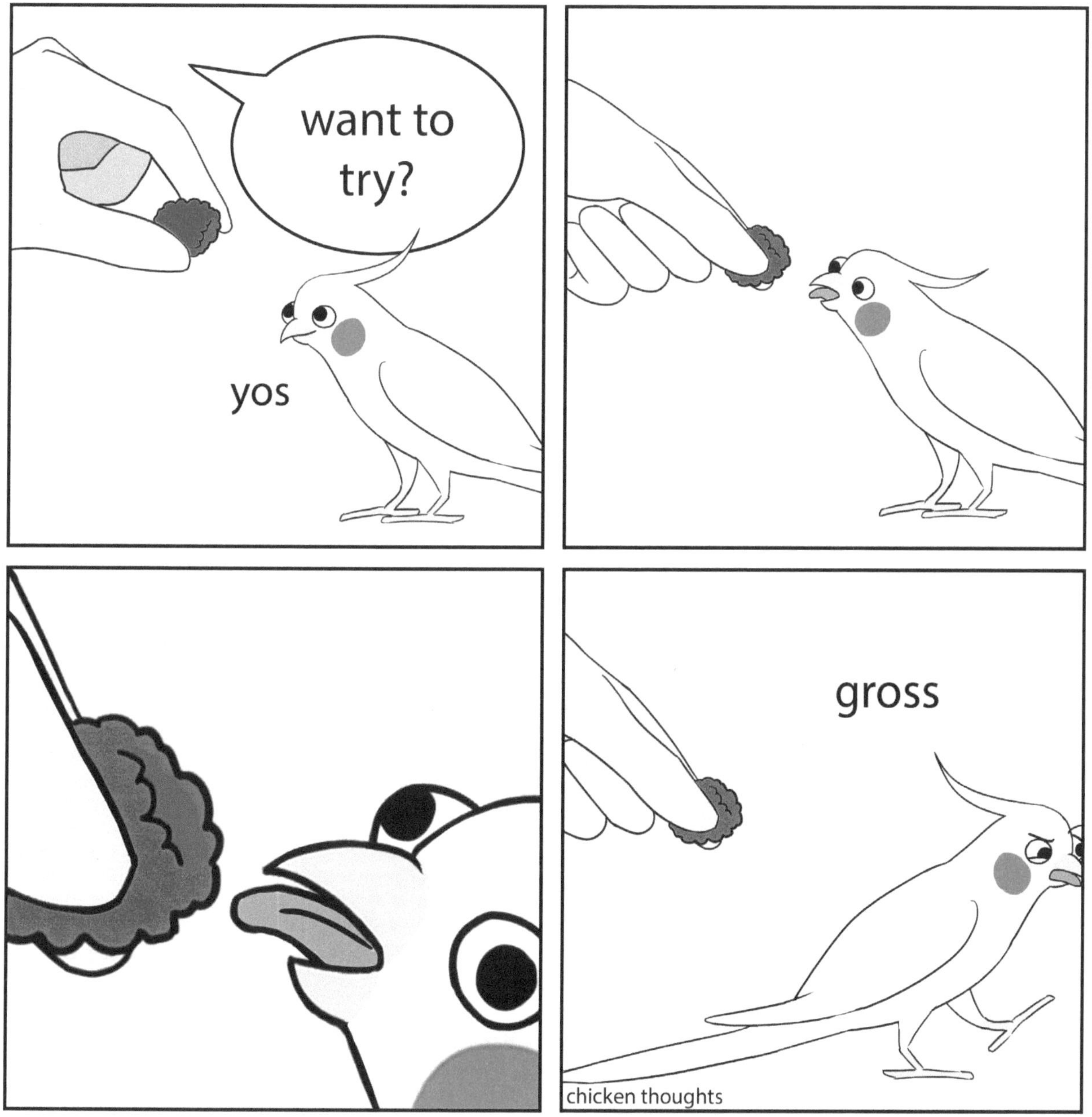
want to try?
yos
gross
chicken thoughts

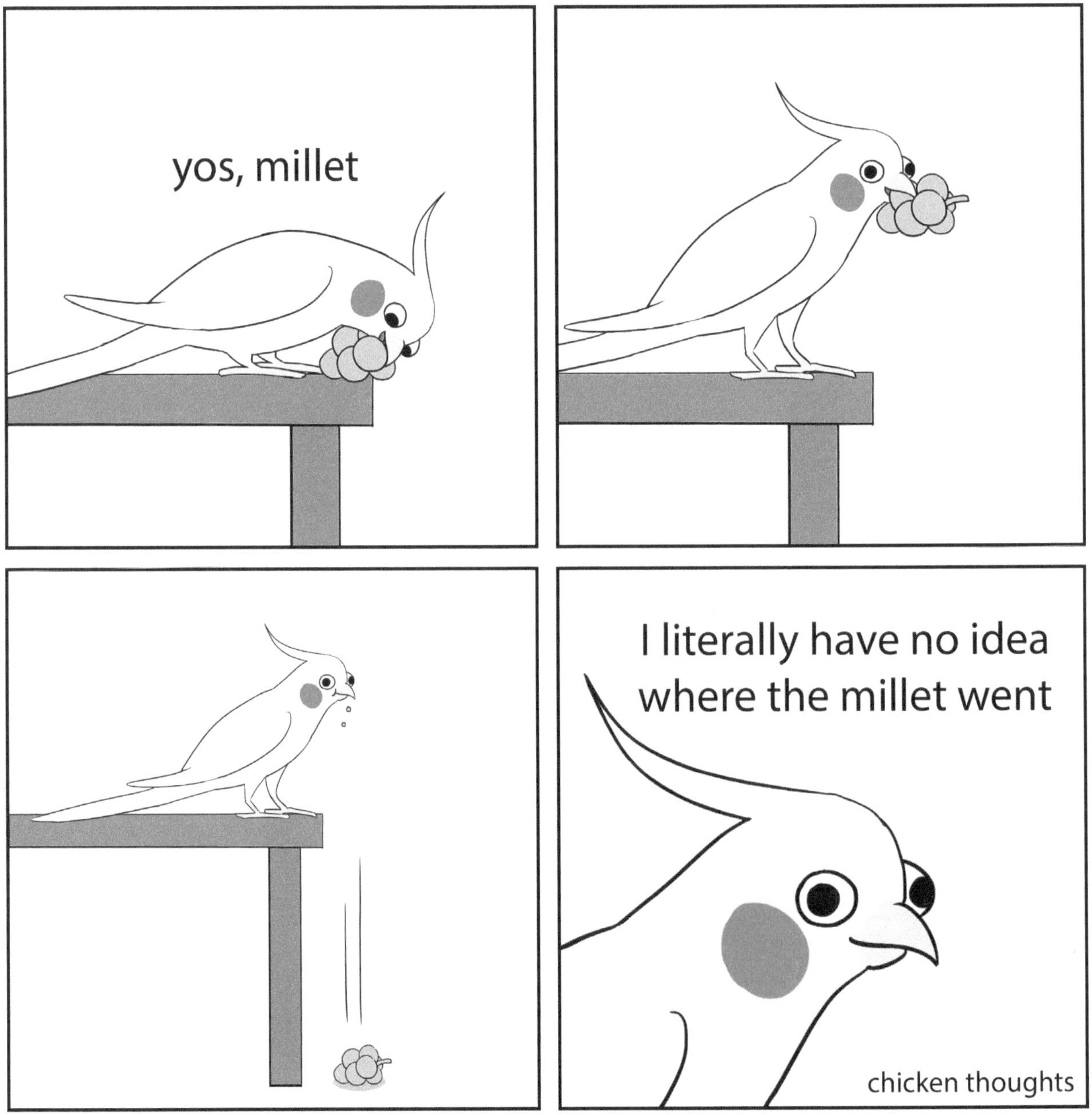
yos, millet
I literally have no idea
where the millet went
chicken thoughts

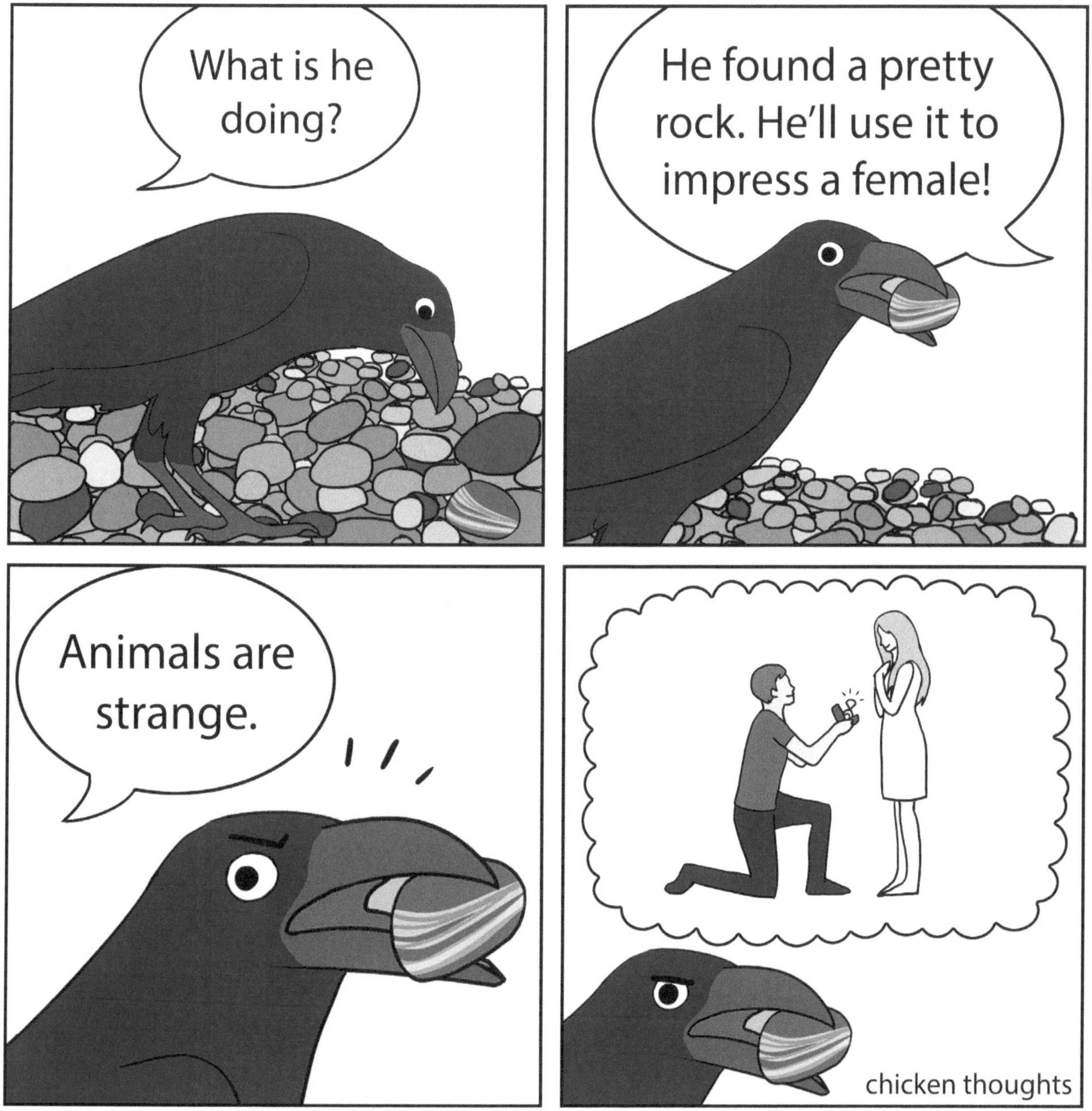
What is he doing?
He found a pretty rock. He'll use it to impress a female!
Animals are strange.
chicken thoughts

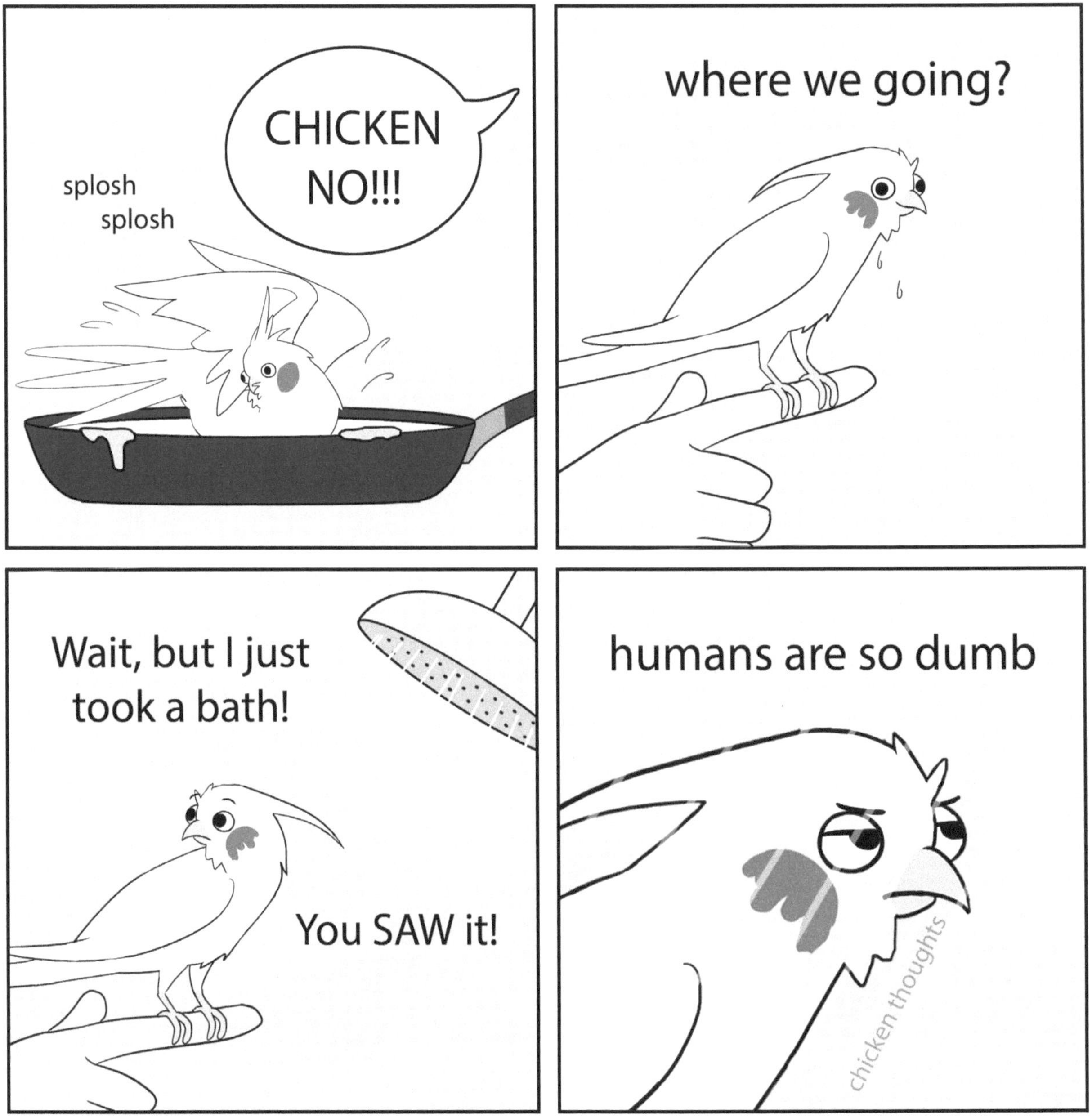
CHICKEN NO!!!
splosh
splosh
where we going?
Wait, but I just took a bath!
You SAW it!
humans are so dumb
chicken thoughts

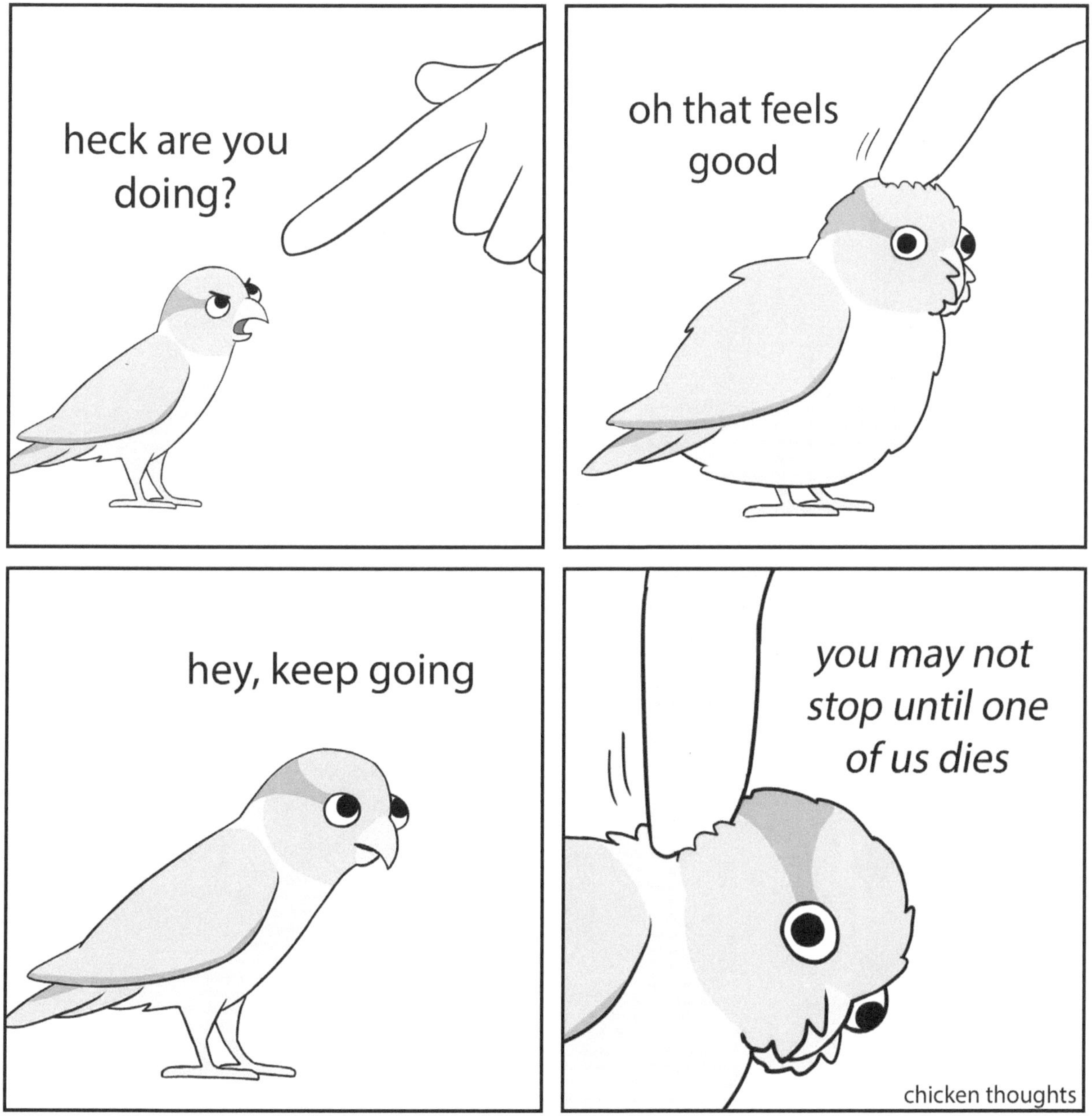
heck are you doing?
oh that feels good
hey, keep going
you may not stop until one of us dies
chicken thoughts

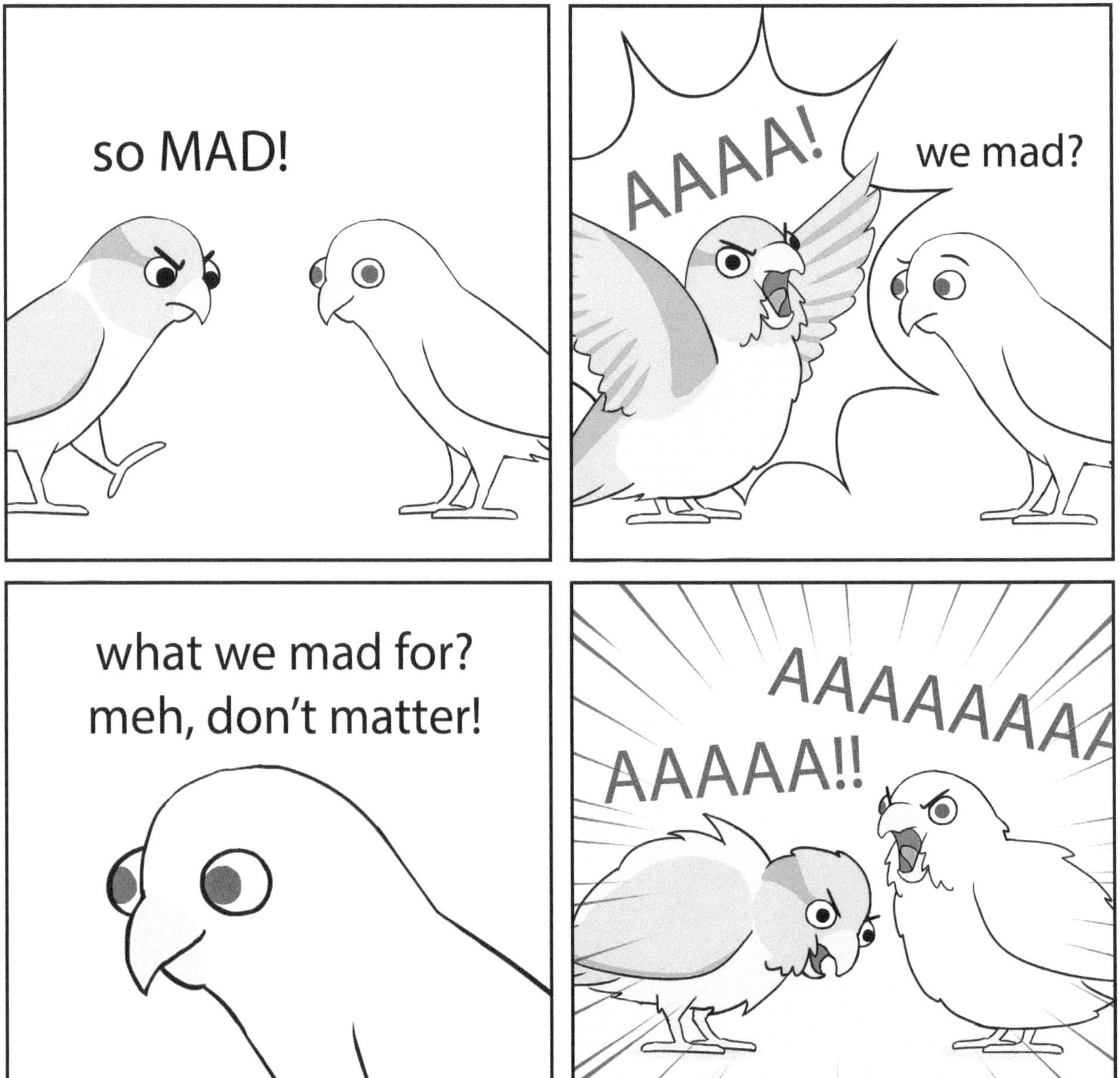
so MAD!
AAAA!
we mad?
what we mad for?
meh, don't matter!
AAAAAAAA
AAAAA!!
chicken thoughts

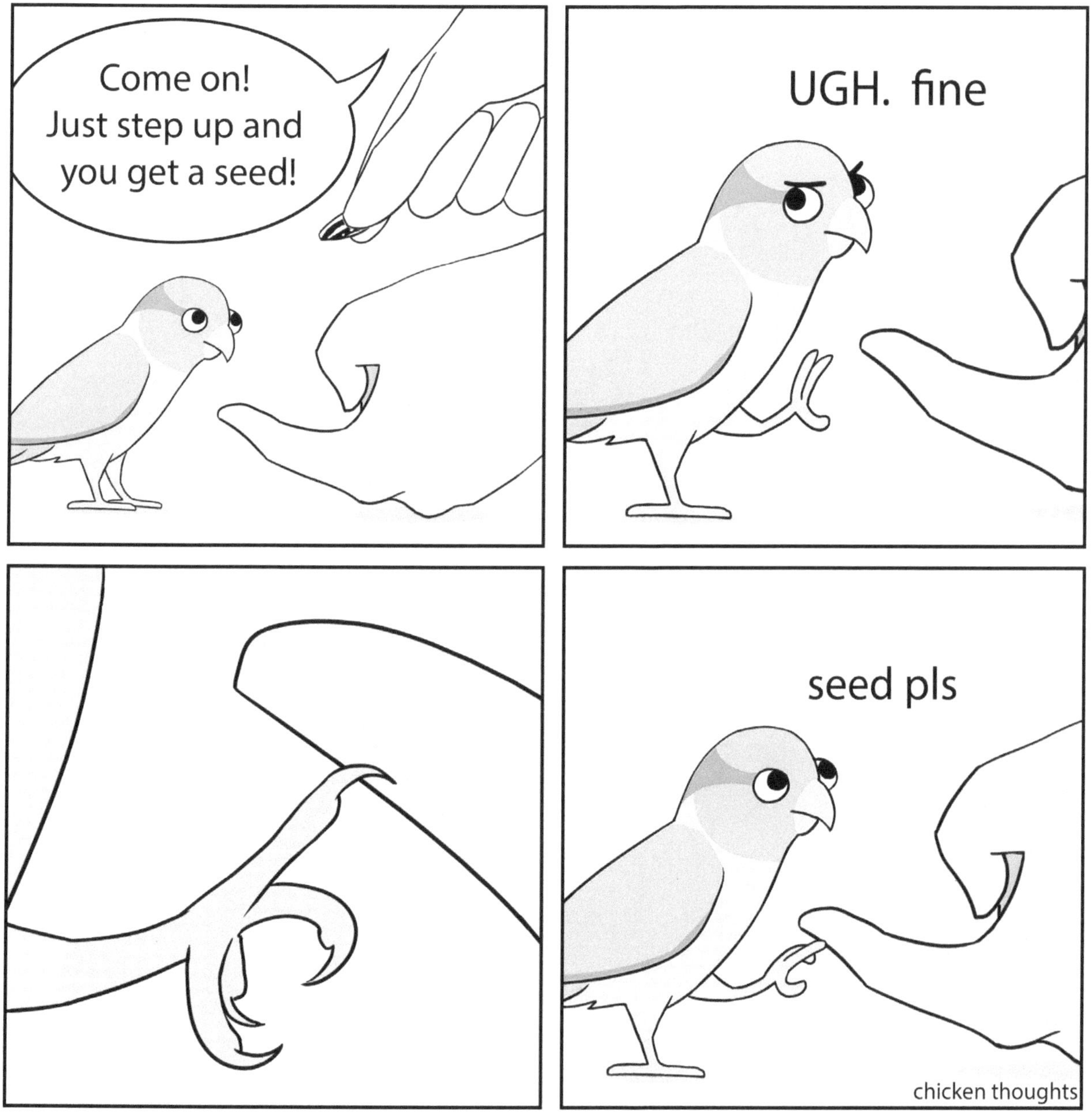
Come on! Just step up and you get a seed!
UGH. fine
seed pls
chicken thoughts

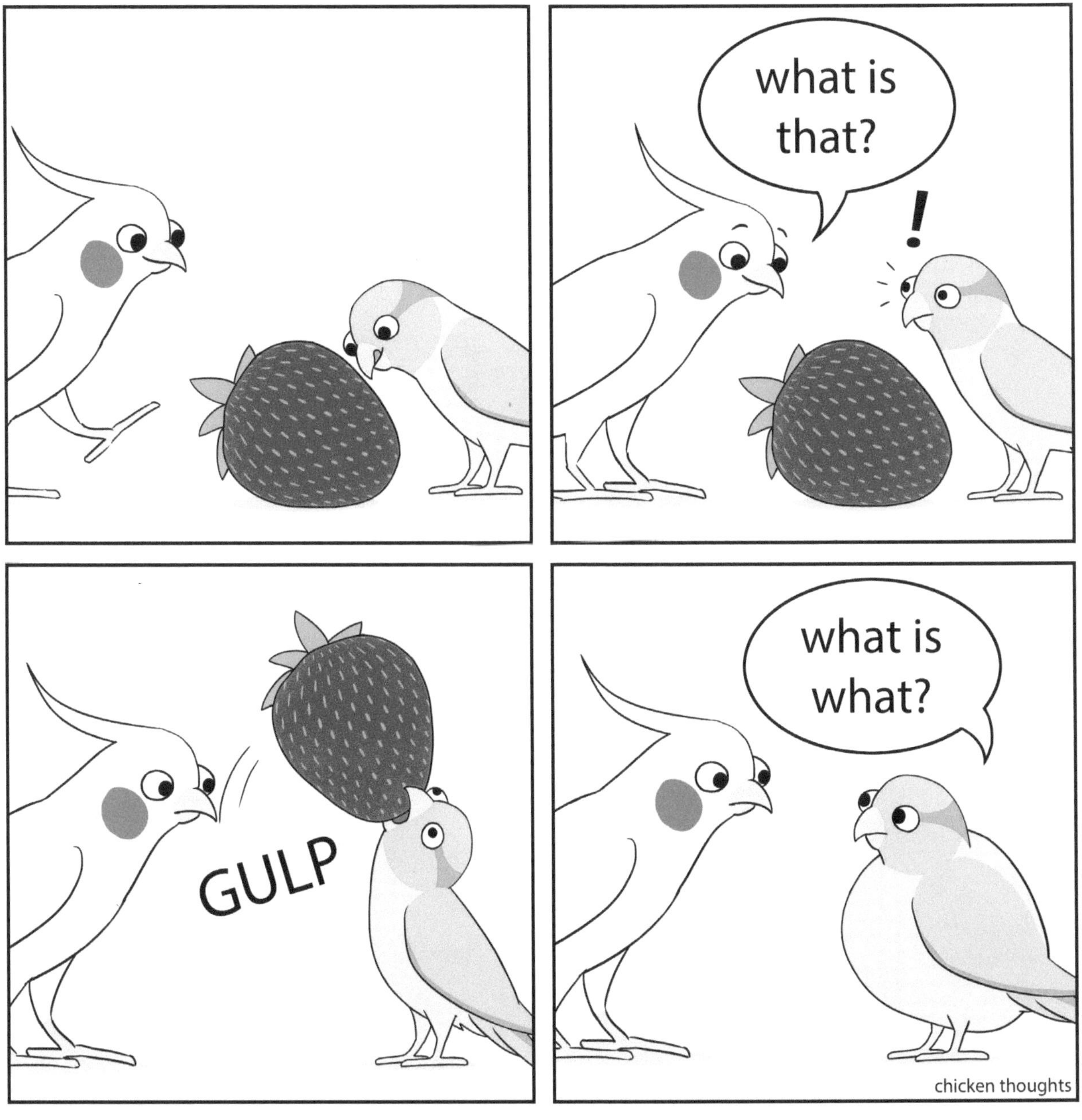
what is
that?
!
GULP
what is
what?
chicken thoughts

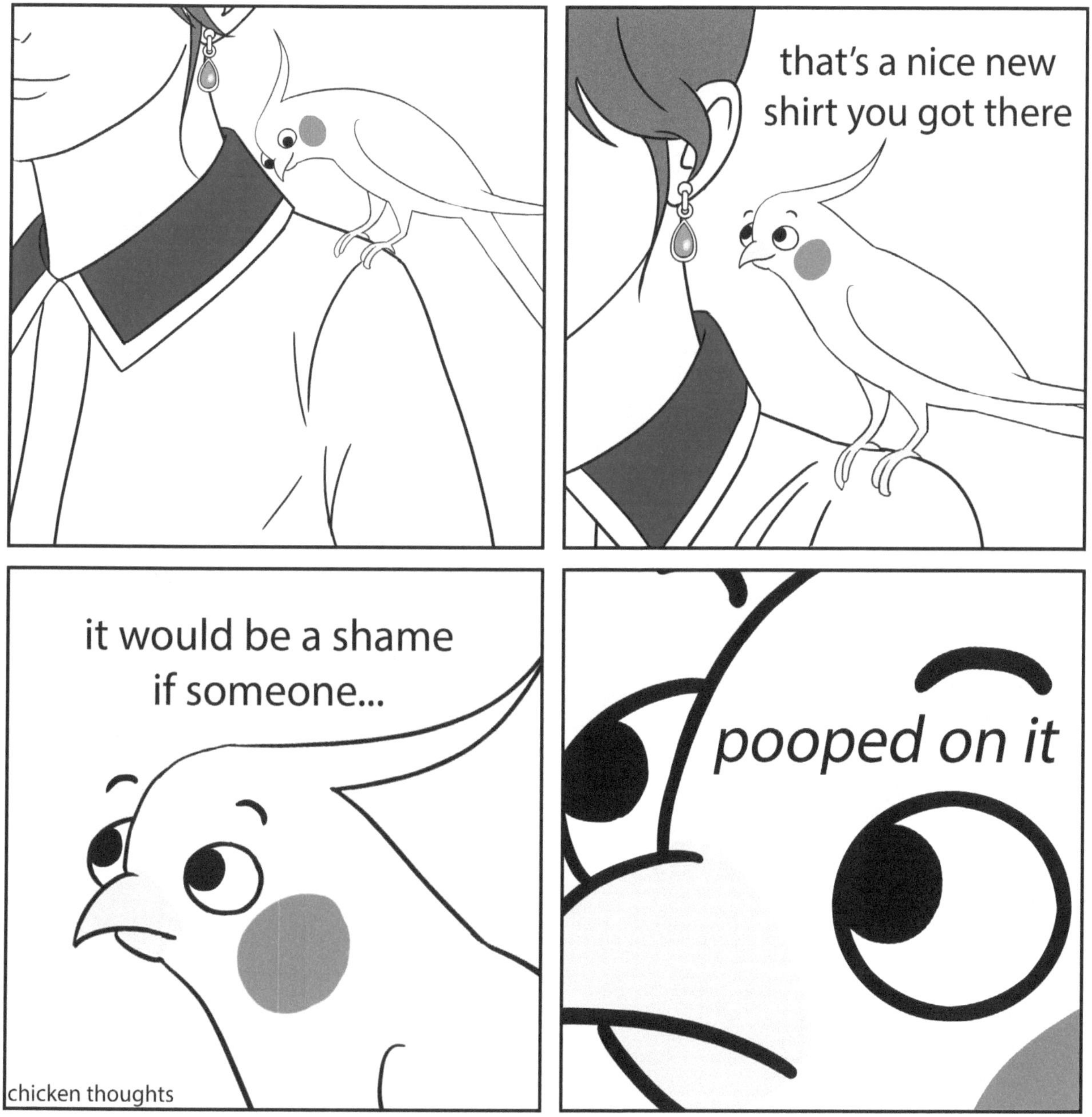
that's a nice new
shirt you got there
it would be a shame
if someone...
chicken thoughts
pooped on it

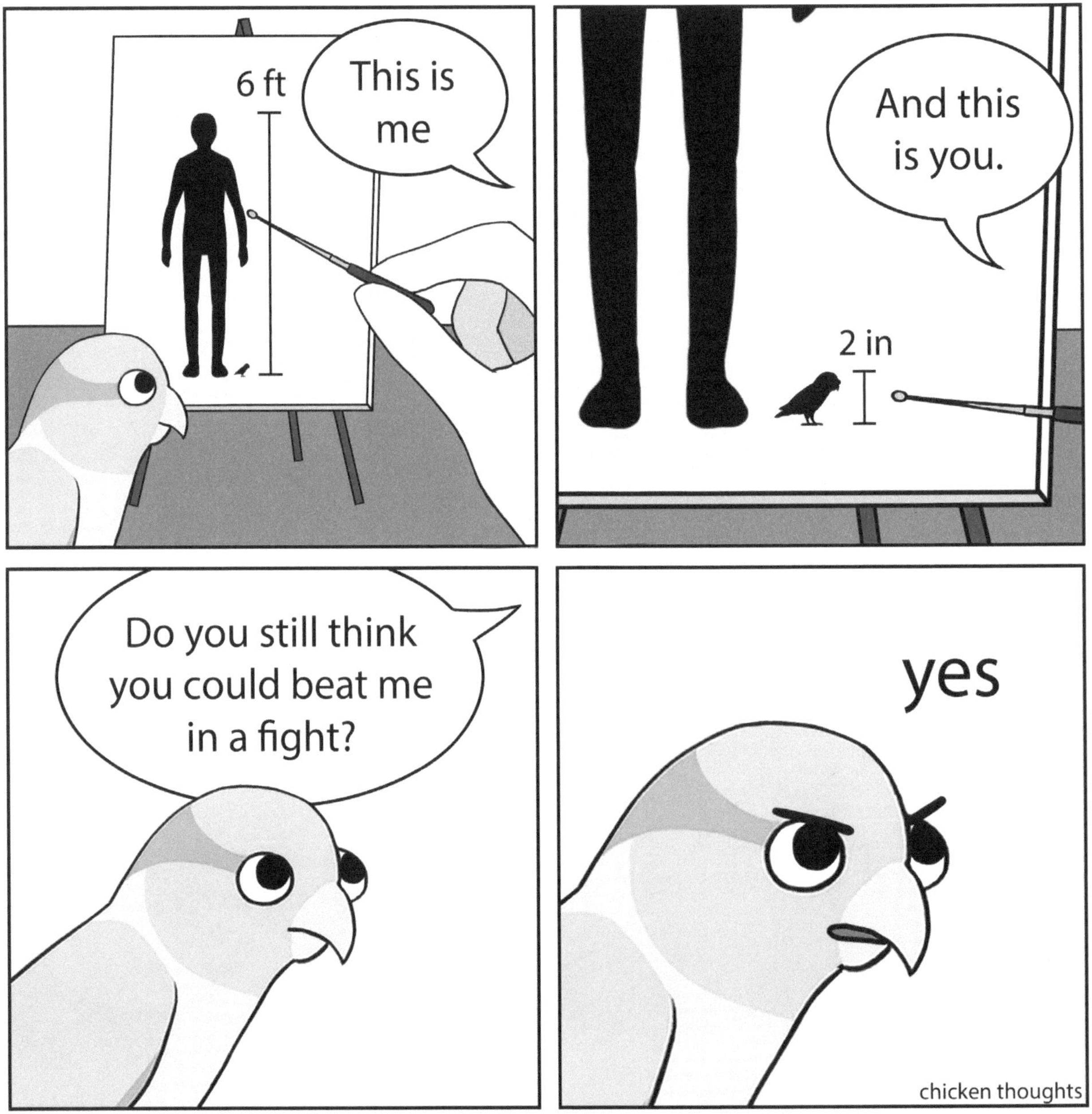
6 ft
This is me
And this is you.
2 in
Do you still think you could beat me in a fight?
yes
chicken thoughts

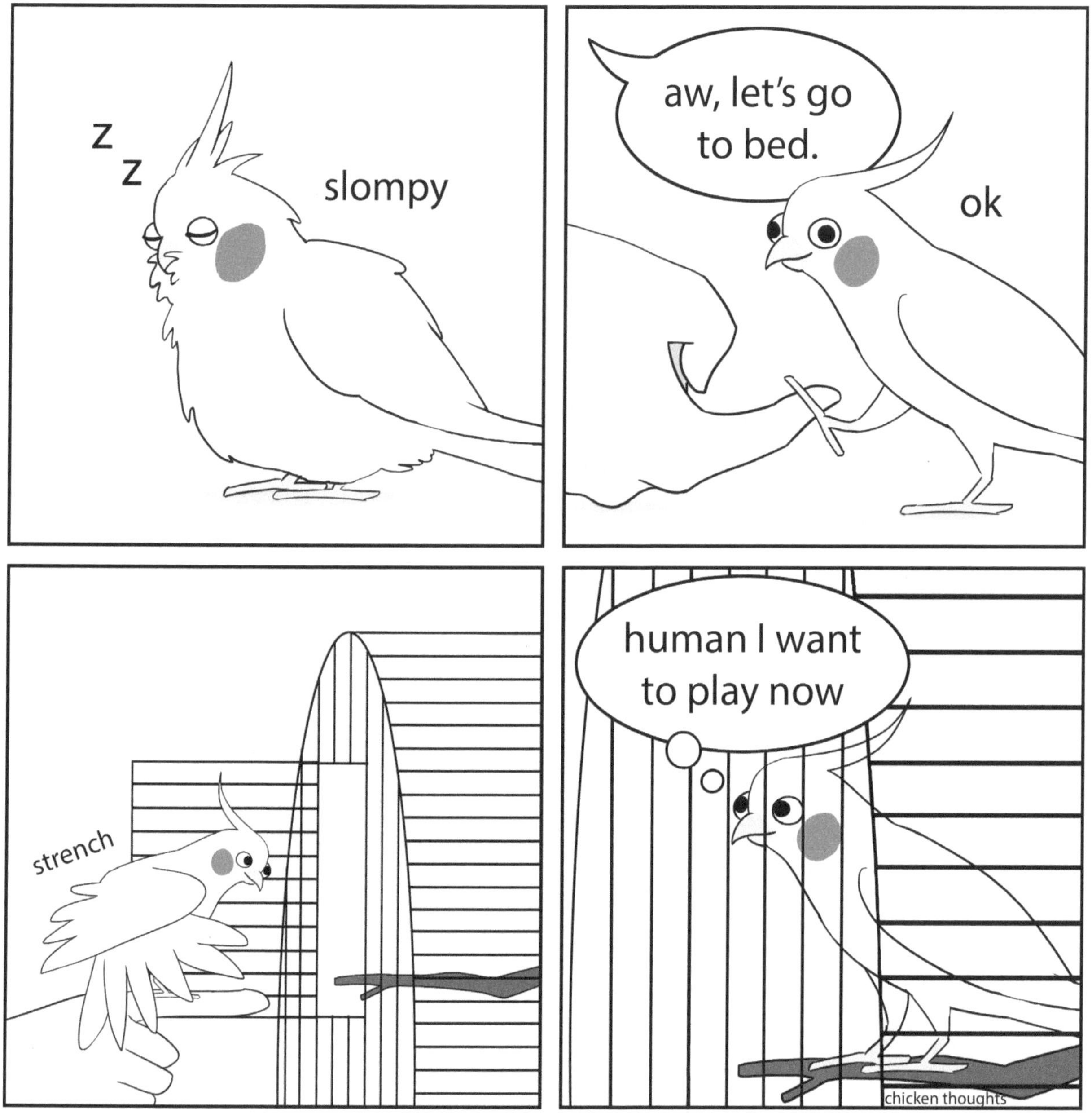
z
z
slompy
aw, let's go
to bed.
ok
strench
human I want
to play now
chicken thoughts

"I visited a parrot shop today and stumbled upon the most wholesome thing. Someone surrendered a little cage to them a while back with like 7 cockatiels stuffed in it. Unfortunately, this bald girl was bullied and plucked to the point that her head feathers will never return.

However, the boy next to her just ended up falling head over heels for her, in all of her bald vulture glory, pair-bonded with her ... So now they just live together there. She said he is constantly feeding and preening her. Everyone deserves [someone] like him in their life."

-Shannon, photographer (@bitisbotanical)

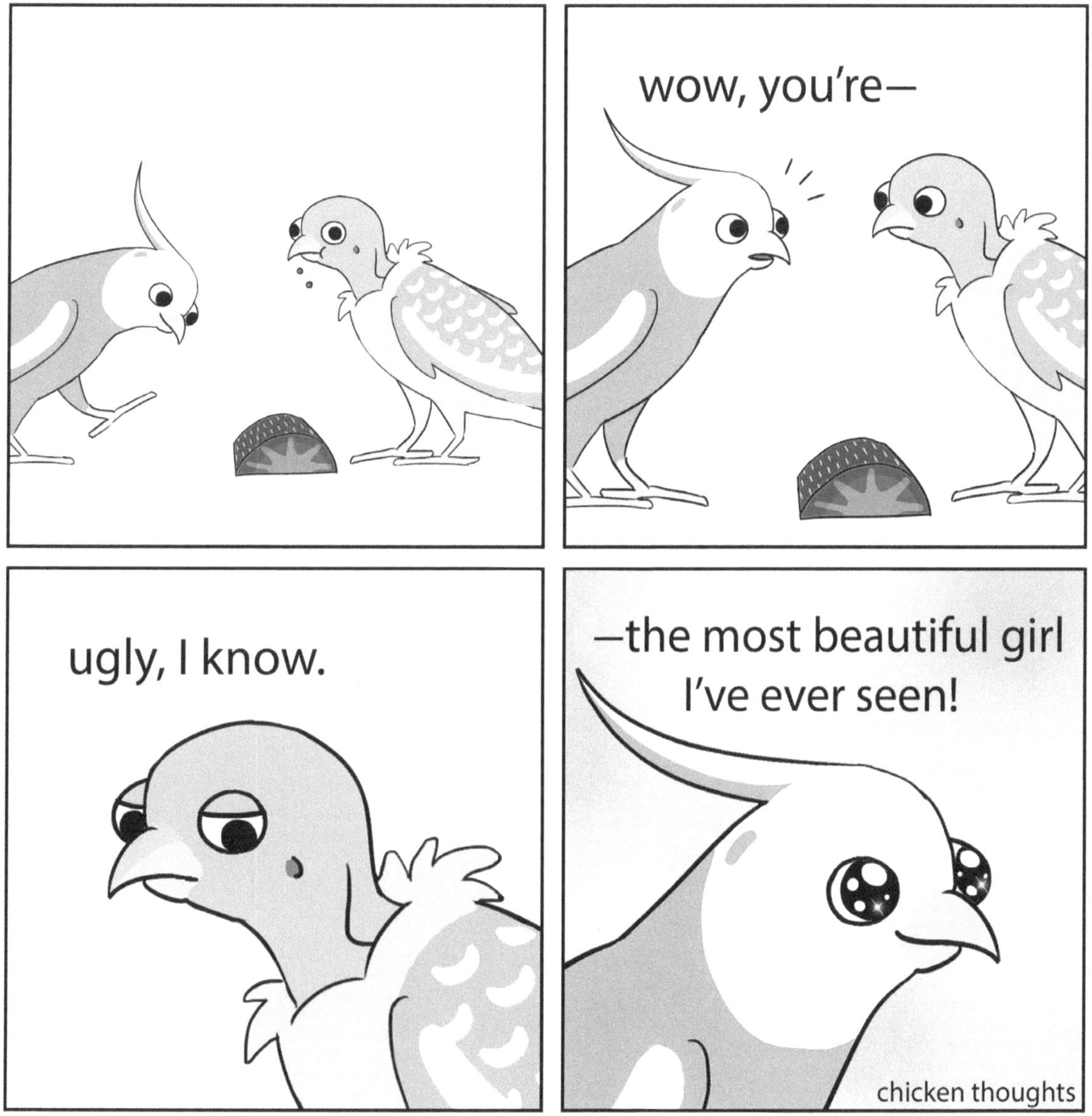
wow, you're–
ugly, I know.
–the most beautiful girl
I've ever seen!
chicken thoughts

The End

CPSIA information can be obtained
at www.ICGtesting.com
Printed in the USA
LVHW071909191020
669184LV00001B/1

* 9 7 8 1 0 8 7 8 8 8 7 3 6 *